Praise for *Bri*

"Before I read *Bridging the God Gap,* I really didn't understand the diversity of thinking that exists among atheists and agnostics. This book changed my attitude and opened up possibilities for healthy communication that didn't exist before. It can be of great help to people seeking to better understand those who see the world differently than themselves and can be especially valuable to families facing strong disagreements over religion."

— Minister, Church of the Brethren

"This book is different from any I have seen and fills a really important gap."

— Theologian John Cobb,
Center for Process Studies

"Finally a book that respects people regardless of whether they are religious. Thought-provoking and even-handed. Thank you for gently nudging your readers into opening their minds – at least a tiny crack."

— Atheist, Palo Alto, California

"The central idea of the book – that atheists, agnostics and theists have more in common than is often believed, and that substantive, rich, meaningful dialogue is not only possible, but necessary – is something that the world sorely needs."

— Rev. Barbara F. Meyers,
Certified Spiritual Director

"*Bridging the God Gap* is well-written, insightful, and chock-full of inspiring, practical wisdom. Getting long-time theological rivals to respect each other as kindred spirits just got a whole lot easier. This book deserves a wide readership. Bravo!"

— Michael Dowd, author of
Thank God for Evolution

Bridging the God Gap

Finding Common Ground
Among Believers, Atheists and Agnostics

Second Edition

Roger Christan Schriner

Living Arts Publications

BRIDGING THE GOD GAP:
  Finding Common Ground Among
  Believers, Atheists and Agnostics
Copyright © 2011 by Roger C. Schriner

Living Arts Publications, Fremont, California
Printed in the United States by CreateSpace.com

Bridging the God Gap draws upon portions of an earlier book, *Do Think Twice.* This second edition replaces *Bridging the Great God Gap*, released May, 2010. Stories about real people have generally been altered to protect privacy.

Library of Congress Control Number: 2011928665
ISBN 978-0-9845840-0-0

By the same author:

Do Think Twice: Provocative Reflections on Age-Old Questions, by Chris Schriner. Creative approaches to topics such as the mystery of consciousness, mind and brain, moral relativism, free will, accepting mortality, theism vs. atheism, the limits of our knowledge, and the mismatch between human nature and the modern world. The book also offers strategies for personal and spiritual growth. The author's contact information is noted above.

Feel Better Now: 30 Ways to Handle Frustration in 3 Minutes or Less, by Christan Schriner, with an Introduction by Ken Keyes. Describes 30 specific techniques for quickly easing distress, and explains how to use these tactics in dealing with everyday pressures and frustrations. Contact Pro-Ed: An International Publisher, 800-897-3202, www.proedinc.com.

Acknowledgments

I appreciate insightful feedback from those who read early drafts of this manuscript (or the previous edition), including Catherine Berthet, David DeLange, Everett DePangher, Dick Duda, Bob Gauntt, David Harris, Stanley Hunt, Hershey Julien, Jo Ann Schriner, and William Schwarz. In addition, the Revs. Steve Clapp, John B. Cobb, Jr., Michael Dowd, Barbara Meyers, Wayne Oates, and Tom Owen-Towle made helpful suggestions from their own faith perspectives.

I am grateful for the guidance of these thoughtful and perceptive commentators. In addition, Chris Lindstrom provided material about the Garrison-Martineau Project and Will Cloughley contributed a moving story about a personal response to the problem of evil.

Most of all I treasure the love, support, and wise counsel of my wife Jo Ann, in labors and laughter, sorrows and delights.

Roger Christan Schriner, April, 2011

Dedicated to the lasting legacy
of Paul Tillich

CONTENTS

Introduction: Building Walls or Building Bridges?

Religion is remarkably effective in bringing people together, but it can be just as powerful in pushing them apart. Consider the frustration and bewilderment expressed in these two conversations:

"I'm sorry Kristen. I know you have to practically drag me out the door to get me to church, but I feel like a hypocrite sitting there listening to the sermon when religion doesn't make sense to me."

"Frank, I'm amazed to hear you say that. We spent months looking for a church that wouldn't push a lot of dogma at us. This congregation seems so open-minded."

"You're right. But these days I don't think I even believe in God."

"I am so sick of you saying she's just going through a phase! Every time she comes home from college she has to talk about why she's become an atheist. This time she gave us a book about 'atheist spirituality.' She won't listen to me, but you're her sister. Can't you talk some sense into her?"

"Dad, you know I've tried. As long as she doesn't try to convert us to her way of thinking I want to let her alone."

In my work as a minister and psychotherapist, I have heard so many people say they hate to discuss religion with family and friends. The conflict between theism and atheism can be particularly hurtful. But as Francis David said hundreds of years ago, "We need not think alike to love alike."

In writing this book about belief and disbelief, I have had several groups of readers in mind. See if you identify with any of the following statements:

❀ *You believe in God,* and you want to communicate with people who doubt that God exists.

❀ *You don't believe in God,* but some of those you care about are committed theists.

❀ *Friends and family members clash about religion.* You wish you could help them reconcile.

❀ *You are in a love relationship* with someone who disagrees with you about theology.

❀ *You aren't sure what you believe,* and you want to reflect about whether there is a God and what God is like.

If you identify with any of these ideas, I hope you will read further. I wrote this book for people like you.

The clash between theism and atheism can also be an internal conflict, when one person has mixed feelings about belief. Many people are confused or ambivalent about God. They can learn to communicate more effectively with *themselves,* moving toward clarity by resolving inner contradictions.

But there is another reason for picking up this book, a reason that is much broader than "theism versus atheism."

❀ You want to have candid and yet respectful conversations with those whose opinions are different from yours – opinions about religion, politics, morality, and other emotionally loaded subjects.

Many of the ideas in *Bridging the God Gap* may be applied to any controversial topic, including partisan politics, gay marriage, sexual ethics, abortion, global warming, and coping with terrorism.

In dealing with such matters we can learn to discuss our disagreements more skillfully. We may also discover that we don't disagree as much as we thought. This book emphasizes both approaches. Theological differences are often less dramatic than they seem, and our real disagreements need not divide us. So in addition to working on person-to-person communication, we will consider why people think God does or does not exist, what God may be like, and how theism and atheism affect our happiness and well-being.

Bridging the God Gap challenges people to be respectful and open-hearted toward those whose opinions are "incorrect." If you choose to continue, I salute you. Many people will shut this book when they realize it might lead them to become more accepting of those whose views they reject.

From time to time you may find yourself hesitating to read any further. In preparing this manuscript I found myself thinking, "Theists won't like that sentence. Atheists will bristle at that remark." But remember, other readers who sharply disagree with your beliefs will be having the same sort of struggle. At least you will have that much in common!

As we will see in Chapter One, arguments about God have intensified in the media recently. Many of us are weary of inflammatory accusations and shrill self-righteousness. Even so, by proposing a cease-fire I know I am inviting attacks from all directions. Stepping into this controversy feels risky, but several life-changing personal experiences have led me to take on this task.

Why I Wrote This Book

I have been interested in religion for almost as long as I can remember. My devout Christian mother encouraged my interest by giving me a five-volume set of Bible stories. Before Mom bought those Bible books, however, I had been reading about biology, zoology, and astronomy. So my impressionable young mind was shaped by two grand visions of reality, the scientific description of the cosmos and the Biblical drama of God and humanity – creation, fall, and redemption. I knew there were inconsistencies between these accounts, but I have always assumed that religion and research data are compatible.

My main vocation has been the Unitarian Universalist ministry. Unitarian Universalism is an unusual religion, partly because it has no fixed theological doctrine. UUs focus on a set of values rather than on a set of beliefs about "how it all is." Unitarian churches welcome a remarkable assortment of viewpoints, from traditional Christians to lifelong atheists. I have needed to address a wide range of belief systems in my sermons and classes, and I have seen that sincere seekers hold many views about deity.

(Even though I am a Unitarian Universalist, this book is not a work of evangelism, and I will seldom refer to my own denomination.)

In addition to ministry, I was a psychotherapist for twenty years. As a therapist I practiced the discipline of trying to understand and appreciate the perspectives of my clients, including their spiritual orientations.

My thoughts about God were also shaped by a difficult life-crisis which turned out to be a splendid opportunity. In my early twenties, I had the remarkable experience of being able to identify with both theism and atheism at the same time. I had grown up with a sense of continuous daily communion with God. In college, however, I began to wonder whether there was anyone present but myself, as I silently sat praying in the University Chapel. As a result, I began to incline toward atheism.

For a while I was so evenly balanced between belief and unbelief that I could see either one with equal clarity. It was as if I were perched high on a mountaintop. If I sat facing east I saw one valley, if I turned west I saw the other, *and both were equally visible.* I could even switch back and forth on purpose. During this time I realized that we can understand ourselves and our world through either theism or atheism. And yet for obvious practical reasons we typically build our personal model of reality on one side of the mountain or the other. People believe or disbelieve in God because that is the only side of the question they can see.

Because of an unusual combination of factors, then, I now think of belief and disbelief as complementary rather than as polar opposites. I do not see any one perspective as having a monopoly on truth, and I find flaws in both theistic and atheistic writings. I have my own views, of course, and I don't claim to be objective. I have done my best to correct for personal biases, and I have flagged sections in which I notice these biases intruding into the text. Nevertheless, I encourage you to read this book reflectively and even critically. Don't just swallow an idea because I express it with great confidence. And if you are committed to some particular religion, please bring your enthusiasm about this faith to *Bridging the God Gap*. When something I have written doesn't seem right to you, remember this principle of the Twelve-Step recovery movement – *"take what works, and leave the rest."*

Preview

In Chapter One I will sketch the current controversy between theism and atheism. Going beyond this conflict requires understanding other viewpoints, so Chapters Two and Three include suggestions about dealing with our own biases. Chapter Four lists strategies for communicating about religion. To focus on human kinship, I will talk about what we all have in common in Chapter Five. Chapters Six and Seven show why the beliefs of theists and atheists are often more similar than they seem. *These two chapters form the heart of this book,* but they cannot be adequately understood without the material that leads up to them. Chapters Eight through Twelve address specific issues that divide believers and non-believers. Then in Chapter Thirteen we will consider disagreements among various forms of theism and various forms of atheism. For example, liberal Christians and fundamentalists argue about how to interpret the Bible. We also find clashes between anti-religious atheists and "spiritual atheists." Chapter Fourteen will synthesize the book's ideas, revealing a whole that is greater than the sum of its parts.

Many of my examples relate to Christian concepts of God, since I am familiar with Christianity. Even so, the book's ideas generally apply to other traditions as well.

Although we'll be discussing serious matters, I hope you won't mind a bit of lightness now and then. A little laughter makes it easier to confront challenging topics, especially when we can laugh at ourselves. You'll also notice that I tend to speak rather personally, and I will sometimes challenge my readers to be personally involved. Any book's benefits will be multiplied if we actively apply its principles. Be on the lookout for whatever is meaningful to you, and think about ways that you can explore the book's ideas and strategies. I will suggest a wide variety of exercises and techniques, which I have placed in shaded boxes marked with this symbol: ✎

To me it would be quite unsatisfying to deal with theology without engaging in personal exploration, and yet I realize that not everyone feels this way. I therefore want to emphasize that all exercises and techniques are optional. Try out some of them, all of them, or none of them, as you prefer. It's completely up to you.

Start Where You Are

Before reading further, I invite you to focus for a few minutes on your own attitudes about God. One way to do that is to make what I call a *radial outline*. To make such an outline, start by writing the name of a topic in the middle of a page. Then list several aspects of this topic, "radiating" from the center like spokes of a wheel. You will find examples below, based upon outlines people have sketched during workshops and counseling sessions.

> ✎ For your first radial outline, begin by writing the word "God" in the center of a blank sheet of paper. Think of different aspects of your opinions about God. These might include whether God exists, what God is like, what has led you to believe or disbe-lieve, arguments in favor of your position, advantages and disadvantages of believing as you do, as well as doubts and confusions. One of the spokes might represent past beliefs. Arrange these in a circle, all around the page, linking them to the central topic with solid lines.

Think about what you might include in your outline before looking at the two examples I have provided. I'll add an agnostic's radial in Chapter Two.

From a theist:

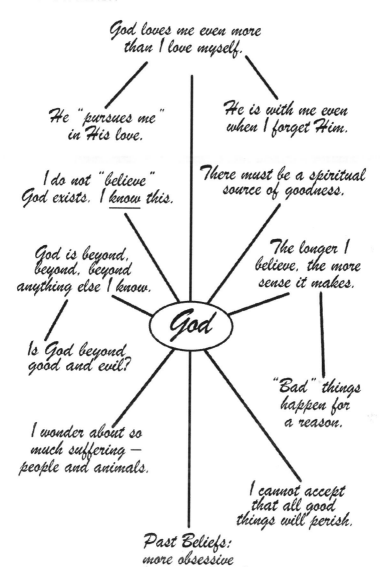

God loves me even more
than I love myself.

He "pursues me"
in His love.

He is with me even
when I forget Him.

I do not "believe"
God exists. I <u>know this.</u>

There must be a spiritual
source of goodness.

God is beyond,
beyond, beyond
anything else I know.

The longer I
believe, the more
sense it makes.

God

Is God beyond
good and evil?

"Bad" things
happen for
a reason.

I wonder about so
much suffering —
people and animals.

I cannot accept
that all good
things will perish.

Past Beliefs:
more obsessive
about little "sins."

From an atheist:

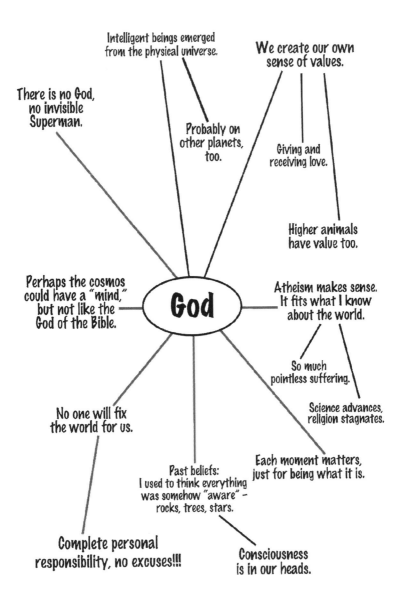

Intelligent beings emerged from the physical universe.

We create our own sense of values.

There is no God, no invisible Superman.

Probably on other planets, too.

Giving and receiving love.

Higher animals have value too.

Perhaps the cosmos could have a "mind," but not like the God of the Bible.

God

Atheism makes sense. It fits what I know about the world.

So much pointless suffering.

Science advances, religion stagnates.

No one will fix the world for us.

Each moment matters, just for being what it is.

Past beliefs: I used to think everything was somehow "aware" – rocks, trees, stars.

Complete personal responsibility, no excuses!!!

Consciousness is in our heads.

What was it like to make your outline? Or if you didn't do it, what might it have been like?

Whatever you write today serves as a partial snapshot of your current beliefs, and you can save it for future reference. If you read this book with an open mind, your radial God-sketch may change by the time you're through. If it does, give yourself credit for having the courage to grow and change. If not, I leave it to you to decide whether you have shown closed-minded resistance or praiseworthy consistency. Most of us have at least a little of both!

Let's begin laying the groundwork for communication and re-conciliation by considering the current controversy between belief and unbelief.

GROUNDWORK

Chapters One through Four:

A Widening Divide
Knowing the Unknowable
God Meets the Mind Machine
Disarming Conversation

Chapter One
A Widening Divide

W hy has the longstanding conflict between theism and atheism intensified lately? First let's consider attitudes toward atheism.

Selfish, Scary, and Strange

When I was a child, I read this definition of "atheist" in *Webster's Unabridged Dictionary:* "A godless person; one who lives immorally as if disbelieving in God."[1] So an official definition in a highly-respected dictionary called atheists immoral.

Many people still think of atheists as deluded and perverse. In 2006 a study compared atheists with other frequently-criticized groups, finding "that Americans rate atheists below Muslims, recent immigrants, gays and lesbians and other minority groups in 'sharing their vision of American society.'" They are "seen as a threat to the American way of life . . . ." To top it all off, "Atheists are also the minority group most Americans are least willing to allow their children to marry."[2]

Penny Edgell, who directed this study, suggests that atheists now play the same role that Catholics, Jews, and Communists played in the past. Belief in God marks a "symbolic moral boundary" that defines who can be considered a good American. "It seems most Americans believe that diversity is fine, as long as every one shares a common 'core' of values that make them trustworthy – and in America, that 'core' has historically been religious."[3] I have certainly seen this in my interfaith work. Over and over I hear that even though we look at life in many different ways, we all believe in God.

Many who responded to Edgell's survey associated non-theism with "criminal behavior . . . rampant materialism and cultural elitism . . . ." (So we are talking about elitist, materialistic criminals. Can't you just picture roving bands of atheists breaking into upscale restaurants, stealing cases of rare old cognac?) Atheists are seen as "self-interested individuals who are not concerned with the common good." Less than half would consider voting for an atheistic Presidential candidate, and that actually shows greater acceptance than in the distant past. Fifty years ago a survey showed that less than 20% would have voted for a well-qualified atheist nominated by their own political party.[4]

No wonder politicians like to speak as if they and God are good buddies. And no wonder many atheists call themselves "humanist" or "agnostic." Humanism is a vague term which is loosely associated with non-belief (as in "secular" humanism). Agnosticism, in religion, means not knowing whether a deity exists. But these terms can also mean, "I'm an atheist but I don't want people to hate me!"[5]

One morning in 2007 I saw an alarming headline in my newspaper: "Stark Gives Confession." The article was about U.S. Rep. Pete Stark. "What is Stark confessing?" I wondered. Embezzlement? X-rated hanky-panky? No. He simply stated that he does not believe in God. If he hadn't been in a solidly safe Congressional seat, that admission could have ended his political career.

As long as people think of atheists as selfish, scary, and strange, it will be impossible to bridge the chasm between believers and nonbelievers. Because I want to help close this gap, I will need to counterbalance stigma and prejudice by defending the legitimacy of unbelief. But I am not trying to prove that atheism is correct, or that theism is correct. I am trying to show that good people can believe either way.

A Few Key Words

When we talk about religion it's easy to react to terminology instead of hearing what others really mean. Richard Dawkins quipped that his parents were "mildly disappointed when I'd said I didn't believe in God any more, but being an *atheist* was another thing altogether."[6] "Atheist" and "atheism" are such thoroughly disparaged labels that even those who reject the idea of a supreme being may refuse to apply these terms to themselves.

To avoid confusion, let me explain how I will use some important words. First of all, I define *theism* very broadly to mean any viewpoint which treats God as a reality rather than as a figment of our imaginations. If someone says God is real instead of imaginary, I will call that person a theist.[7] This understanding of theism includes monotheism, polytheism, deism, pantheism, and panentheism.[8]

I consider people to be *agnostics* if they are ambivalent about whether any sort of deity exists. I consider people *atheists* if they reject both traditional and non-traditional ideas of deity.[9] Because it is a stigmatized term, some readers who fit this description will not want to call themselves atheists, and that's fine. We are all free to define words as we see fit, as long as we make our own meaning clear to others.

Lifestance is a relatively new term for "A framework of ideas that helps us understand the world and find meaning and value in life."[10] Both religious and non-religious perspectives could qualify as lifestances.

By the way, the question of whether God exists can become clouded by the fact that people talk about existence in several different ways. As we will see in Chapter Eight, some theologians say God is beyond all human concepts of existence or non-existence. As I use this term, however, God "exists" if God is real instead of fictional. Theologian John Haught puts it well: "If faith in God is truthful, then, as the new atheists rightly point out, there must be something in reality that corresponds to the idea of God."[11]

A History of Hostility

Hatred of atheists goes back for millennia, and calling someone an atheist has been a way of mocking those whose religious views are unfashionable. In ancient days, for example, Jews and Christians were scorned as atheists because they rejected pagan gods and goddesses.[12]

It wasn't until the nineteenth century that atheism became intellectually acceptable. The door to disbelief swung open after Charles Darwin suggested that evolution rather than miraculous creation might account for animal variety, from hummingbirds to humpback whales. Till Darwin almost all well-educated people thought the only way to explain the diversity of living creatures was to assume an intelligent designer.

Communication between believers and unbelievers has sometimes been respectful. Haught offers several examples, as does Karen Armstrong.[13] In recent years, however, many American religious leaders have sharply attacked non-believers. This is not surprising, since public opinion in the U.S. is increasingly polarized. Talk show hosts on both the right and the left know that ranting against an "enemy" boosts ratings. Political strategists use negative advertising to mobilize voters, stirring up fear and revulsion.

"Humanists are the mortal enemy of all pro-moral Americans, and the most serious threat to our nation in its entire history,"[14] declared the Rev. Tim LaHaye, a prominent Christian minister and co-author of the *Left Behind* series of novels about the end of the world. And in 1987, President George H. W. Bush stated, "I don't know that atheists should be considered as citizens, nor should they be considered patriots. This is one nation under God."[15]

By comparison, listen to his son, President George W. Bush: "The great thing about America . . . is that you should be allowed to worship any way you want. And if you choose not to worship, you're equally as patriotic as somebody who does worship."[16] Despite the current drift toward polarization, the long run trend is toward seeing non-believers as ordinary human beings rather than malevolent misfits. Thus it is not surprising that the younger Bush seems more open-minded about religion than his dad.

When doubters keep silent about their skepticism they are able to "pass," allowing others to assume they are conventional believers. As a result, many theists have no idea that their good friends are atheists or agnostics. Their attitudes toward non-believers may reflect simple stereotypes, based upon media portrayals of outspoken anti-religious atheists. As Edgell puts it, "Americans *construct the atheist* as the symbolic representation of one who rejects the basis for moral solidarity and cultural membership in American society altogether."[17]

While I was working on this manuscript, an atheist sent a letter to our local newspaper criticizing Christmas. Another fellow replied to this letter, and stereotyped all atheists as showing "hatred, disdain, intolerance, and lack of respect."[18] This was a fine example of "constructing the atheist" as a cartoon-like fantasy figure. When we don't know much about some group of people, it's easy to make up stories about what they are like.

Turning to the other end of the religious spectrum, people also stereotype conservative Christians, often known as evangelicals. I have heard them dismissed as ignorant, rigid, narrow-minded yokels. And yet many self-described evangelicals are thoughtful and well-informed. They also vary enormously in their beliefs. For example, a recent study showed that "roughly one-in-ten white evangelicals believes in reincarnation" and 13% believe in astrology,[19] which are certainly not orthodox Christian doctrines. We cannot be summed up by simple labels.

The New Atheism

Several non-believers have now returned fire, writing anti-theistic books such as *The God Delusion,* by Richard Dawkins, *The End of Faith,* by Sam Harris, and *God Is Not Great,* by Christopher

Hitchens. Dawkins lays out detailed arguments against belief in God. Harris attacks the whole notion of faith, even as practiced by religious moderates. The subtitle of Hitchens' book is *How Religion Poisons Everything.* All of them deplore both religious belief and the evil deeds of institutional religion.

Although philosopher Daniel Dennett is sometimes lumped together with Harris, Dawkins, and Hitchens, he is less consistently anti-religious. He doesn't hesitate to skewer traditional doctrines, but he also compliments churchgoers for feeding the hungry and caring for the sick.[20]

At times the new atheists make factual and logical errors, but they are smart and passionate people who care about our human future. For a clear and readable overview of a case for atheism, I recommend Dawkins' *The God Delusion.* The book has sold around two million copies, translated into over 30 languages. For examples of church-supported cruelty, read *The End of Faith,* Chapter Three. Hitchens' fourth chapter, "A Note on Health, to Which Religion Can Be Hazardous," includes eye-popping examples such as African mullahs telling their congregations that the polio vaccine is a Western plot to sterilize Muslims.[21]

Although I agree with many of the new atheists' critiques of religion, I am uncomfortable when some of them seem to claim intellectual superiority. After all, many religious traditionalists possess powerful intellects and vast knowledge. "What is most repellent about the new atheism," writes literary critic James Wood, "is its intolerant certainty . . . ."[22]

The ink had hardly dried on new-atheist manifestos when believers replied with a sort of new anti-atheism. John Haught indicts recent atheist writings as "shallow and inaccurate," calling Dawkins' discussion of the Bible "a remarkable display of ignorance and foolish sarcasm."[23] James P. Carse condemns them for attacking "a hasty caricature." "Typically, the god unbelievers are rejecting is one found nowhere within the living religions."[24] Karen Armstrong charges them with having "an extremely literalist notion of God. For Dawkins, religious faith rests on the idea that *'there exists a superhuman, supernatural intelligence, who deliberately designed and created the universe and everything in it.'*"[25] She maintains that this concept is woefully out of date.[26]

Atheists could reply that if Armstrong is correct, even liberal congregations are chock-full of literalists. Believing that God designed and created the universe is middle-of-the-road Christianity, not extreme literalism. Although many theologians no longer think of God as a super-powerful being, Armstrong admits that contemporary theology has "rarely reached the pews."[27]

Despite the claim that traditional Christian beliefs are obsolete, many such beliefs are widely accepted, at least in the United States. According to public opinion polls, 80% of Americans believe in miracles[28] and about 80% of American Christians believe that Jesus will return to Earth.[29] "A new poll from the Pew Research Center finds that roughly four in 10 Americans believe the Second Coming will happen by 2050."[30] Sociologist of religion Rodney Stark suggests that most believers see God as a supernatural conscious being, because "only divine beings *do* anything" and "the supernatural is the only plausible source of many benefits we greatly desire."[31]

I cannot ignore millions of churchgoers as if they do not count, nor can I criticize atheistic writers for addressing doctrines which are accepted by most of their fellow citizens.

Another charge against the new atheists is that they see religion as merely a matter of affirming certain intellectual propositions, such as the claim that God is an invisible super-being. Since religion is a response of the whole person rather than just the logical, intellectual aspects of the mind, atheists are attacking the wrong target.

I agree that religion is much more than theology, but any passionate commitment, including religious faith, is thoroughly entangled with beliefs about the way things are. Suppose you are engaged to be married. It might seem as if your romance is simply an affair of the heart, but love always involves beliefs about facts. Wouldn't you feel a bit nervous if you were confronted with evidence that the object of your affections does not exist? "What? My fiancé is an actor pretending to be someone else?" Such a possibility would surely impact your relationship. Similarly, the question of whether God actually exists bears directly on whether faith in God continues.

So we need to use our heads. On the other hand, some atheists do seem to overemphasize reason and science. One secular humanist told me that he lives his whole life on the basis of scientifically-validated data. I asked him how science could validate the common-sense judgment that love is typically better than hate. Setting up studies to prove this truism would be a Herculean task.

Here's another legitimate criticism: Some atheists seem to think that by poking holes in one kind of theism they have destroyed all basis for belief in any sort of god. Rebutting every idea of god would take many volumes, but it would be helpful if a well-known atheist could analyze even one or two highly sophisticated theologies, such as those of Scotty McLennan and Eric Reitan.

McLennan is chaplain at Stanford University. In *Jesus Was a Liberal* he writes that "God is the infinite and the eternal; God is the law and order of the universe; God is the spirit that infuses all life; and God is love." However he does not see God as having a particular plan "for anyone or anything beyond the magnificent natural order of the universe, including all of its natural laws." This approach is immune to the standard atheist objection that God is only a wish-fulfilling father figure.[32]

Philosopher Eric Reitan's thoughtful and readable book, *Is God a Delusion?* sharply criticizes atheistic writings but tries to be fair-minded. Reading Reitan would be an excellent way for an atheist or agnostic to see how someone with keen intelligence, wide-ranging knowledge, and a fine moral sense could believe in a personal God.

Other theologians with sophisticated concepts of God include Mark Johnston and John Cobb.[33] I also recommend Karen Armstrong's *A History of God* and *The Case for God,* which highlight the richness and complexity of the world's spiritual traditions.

Can We Talk?

Some writers are now encouraging respectful dialogue between theists and atheists. The Rev. Tom Owen-Towle favors an approach "that applauds critical piety, trustful uncertainty, and skeptical believing as complementary attitudes to juggle during the religious journey."[34] McLennan, Reitan, Cobb, Owen-Towle, Dennett, Ian S. Markham,[35] and the Rev. William Murry[36] are examples of writers who persuasively advocate their own viewpoints without demonizing those who disagree.

One remarkable story of positive communication involves a nineteenth-century anti-slavery activist, William Lloyd Garrison, and Harriet Martineau, a novelist and sociologist. After Martineau espoused atheism, Garrison (a committed Christian) wrote her a respectful and supportive letter. He assured Martineau that "your skepticism . . . has never altered my confidence in the goodness of your heart and the nobleness of your character . . . ."[37]

Inspired by their example, Chris Lindstrom organized the Garrison-Martineau Project in 2003. As she writes in a Garrison-Martineau brochure,

"The so-called 'culture war' in this country has separated Garrisons and Martineaus for too long. Listen to the words of everyday folks like yourself, both atheist and Christian, who have written to me."

'I hope there are people like me out there . . . It feels as if I should really hide what I'm thinking because it's just plain dangerous. Or should I fake that I'm believing in whatever god just to have a normal life?' – Dave

'I'm not sure what the purpose of the atheist is in working to restrict the freedom of the majority for the benefit of a very small minority.' – Bill

For several years the Garrison-Martineau Project gathered small groups of atheists and believers to "see everyone else at the table as human beings with human concerns which must be addressed."[38] Over 200 people participated in the program. This is a fine example of appreciating each other's humanity instead of distancing each other through shallow stereotypes. We need this sort of face-to-face communication and I hope this book contributes to many such conversations.

> *Summing up:* For centuries atheists have been reviled as misguided and immoral. Although skepticism about deity has become somewhat more acceptable in recent decades, unbelievers are still strongly stigmatized. Some atheists have responded with attacks on traditional religion, but many commentators are now saying it's time for a cease-fire.

With this background in mind we can begin considering ways that theists and atheists can accept and even appreciate each other. I will offer many suggestions, but my project of reconciliation depends primarily on twelve key ideas. **I will boldface each key idea and mark it with this symbol:** ❖

Most of these twelve ideas are simple and even obvious, but if we fully unpack their implications we will discover a hidden kinship between belief and unbelief. The first of these ideas appears early in the next chapter, and you will encounter ten out of the twelve by the end of Chapter Seven.

Chapter Two
Knowing the Unknowable

One morning I began my Sunday sermon by asking, *"What is the most popular religion in the world?"* But that was a trick question, because I wasn't looking for the name of some far-flung ecclesiastical empire with billions of followers. I think the world's most popular religion is an unnamed faith, a secret religion which is even more widely embraced than the adoration of power and money. As I see it:

❖ **The world's most popular religion is**
the worship of our own opinions.

The creed that sings in the hearts of millions of Christians, Jews, Muslims, Buddhists, Hindus, and atheists is the passionate conviction that *"I'm right!"* – the reverence for our own beliefs.

Although I'm-rightism is clearly popular, people who worship their own ideas are rather shy about discussing their true devotion. And there's an awkward reality which undermines this hidden religion – we can't all be right. Nevertheless it is easy to be cheerfully confident that we are correct and others are mistaken.

One way that we idolize our own conceptions is by confusing our ideas about deity with deity itself. That is as absurd as thinking we could eat the idea of a sandwich, but avoiding this blunder is oddly difficult. People prostrate themselves before some beloved word-picture of God as if it were the Ultimate. I agree with Eric Reitan that "faith in this sense is idolatrous. It involves devotion to one's own concept of God rather than to the truth about God."[39]

In writing this book I have tried to set aside my own biases, but one strong conviction of mine will be blazingly obvious: I think it is extremely hard for human beings to understand something as mysterious and profound as God (or Ultimate Reality). Perhaps you are more optimistic than I am about our ability to comprehend the

Ultimate. In that case you may disagree with some of the things I say about the limits of human knowledge, and that's perfectly all right. Remember, take what works for you, and leave the rest.

Let's Pretend We All Agree

The love of our own beliefs has tempted religions toward dogma and conformity. Because we revere our opinions, we want these opinions to be applauded. We therefore find others who will pat us on the back and tell us we're right, and we happily return the favor. As a result, churches that turn themselves into mutual-validation societies can attract lots of members.

By focusing on a creed, a holy book, or a particular set of traditions, congregations can manufacture the illusion of unity: "We are all marching in the same direction. We all believe in the same great story." These words are comforting but frequently false. Within Christianity, for example, some follow a god of love while others focus so much on divine wrath that divine compassion seldom crosses their minds. Isn't it astounding that a neo-Nazi can claim to follow Jesus, "the Prince of Peace?" Two people may point to the same book without pointing to the same truth.

Fortunately some spiritual communities refuse to fabricate pseudo-unanimity. Instead, they encourage both children and grownups to think for themselves.[40] I think of a motto of the United Church of Christ: "God is still speaking." And not all religions emphasize that they are right and others are wrong. A recent survey asked people whether their religion is the only true faith. Eighty percent of Jehovah's Witnesses said yes. So did 36 percent of evangelicals and 33 percent of Muslims. By contrast, about 90 percent of Hindus, 86 percent of Buddhists, and 82 percent of Jews do not think theirs is the only valid path."[41] And notice this: Even though many evangelicals and Muslims say theirs is the one true religion, over half of their fellow congregants deny this claim. This is another reminder that we shouldn't stereotype each other.

Just as believers may belong to congregations of like-minded people, many non-believers participate in secular communities of agreement which confirm their skeptical convictions. For example, at one time very few academic philosophers affirmed traditional concepts of God. Philosophers sometimes took it for granted that no intellectually sophisticated person would believe in supernatural entities. Interestingly, theism in general and Christianity in particular are now endorsed by many young philosophers, disturbing what was once a strong community of agreement.[42]

Both theists and atheists have found ways of explaining why they are so sure of themselves about theology. Theists often say that even though our minds are fallible, we know the supreme being through special revelation. Thanks to God's self-disclosure, we grasp hidden truths which we could never have discovered on our own. But here's the problem: Even though a deity could reveal itself to us, it's up to us to interpret this revelation. Christianity in particular has emphasized revelation through Holy Scripture, but we are responsible for deciding what Scripture means. And Christianity has fragmented into over 30,000 denominations, frequently splitting over disagreements about how to interpret the Bible. Evidently we have a lot of trouble figuring out what the Holy Spirit is trying to tell us. Besides, members of non-Christian religious communities also sincerely believe that their doctrines were delivered by God. So who's right? (Why we are, of course!)

Like believers, atheists also like to feel certain that they are correct. To justify dogmatic disbelief, they sometimes think their intelligence and educational level make them superior to those gullible folks who go to church. But lots of people who are smart and well-informed accept traditional religion. There are Nobel laureates who believe, and high school dropouts who disbelieve. And some highly-educated atheists reject deity for reasons that are mainly emotional rather than intellectual.

Could I Be Wrong?

People want trustworthy answers to life's big questions, but our craving for certainty makes it harder to understand another person's perspective.

❖ **In building bridges to those**
whose opinions contrast with your own,
you may confront an unsettling possibility:
They might be right.

Are you strongly attached to many of your religious or philosophical beliefs? Well, so am I. So we will continue to be. Reading this book will not eradicate the I'm-right bias. But we can learn to see glimmers of truth in the seemingly peculiar ideas of friends and family members.

> ✎ Here is an exercise in open-mindedness: Think of some philosophy of life that you consider false, and ask yourself questions such as these:
> ✸ Am I smarter than *everyone* who believes it?
> ✸ Am I morally superior to *all* of its adherents?
> ✸ Do I think I know important facts that *every one of them* has overlooked?

If you could not answer yes to these questions, is there any good reason for being absolutely certain that you are correct? *(And remember that I am also challenging readers who disagree with you about theology: What makes them assume that you are deluded?)*

Religious teachers have sometimes rebuked their followers for making themselves right in their own eyes, focusing on other people's errors and overlooking their own. "Why do you see the speck that is in your brother's eye, but do not notice the log that is in your own eye? Or how can you say to your brother, Let me take the speck out of your eye, when there is the log in your own eye?"[43] As the Muslim Ibn al-Arabi put it, *"Everyone praises what he believes; his god is his own creature, and in praising it he praises himself."*[44]

Part of the problem is that new ideas disturb interlocking patterns of opinions that fit together like houses made of bricks. Suppose somebody says, "You should take out *that* brick and replace it with *this* one which looks much better." Even if it's the finest brick ever baked, it may have an unusual shape. To use it, you'd have to dismantle the old structure and reassemble it in a new configuration. Similarly, when we encounter a stimulating new idea about some ethical, social, or religious issue, we examine this "brick" to see if it fits what we already have in place. If not, we throw it away.

Our minds, then, tend to act as closed systems. As Rabbi Steven Reuben commented, "the only person in the world who really likes change is a wet baby."[45]

Charles Taliaferro observes that "For a skeptic to consider the merits of Christianity or for a Christian to consider the merits of atheism can seem like an individual considering whether he or she should become a different person."[46] We need to acknowledge how threatening it is to undermine another person's viewpoint, and realize that we cannot hope to totally change someone's mind about religion in a single conversation. What we can do is try to plant a little seed in the other person's awareness and hope it will grow. And in fairness, we can also allow our friend to plant seeds within us.

Trapped in a prison of self-justifying beliefs, how can we let in some air and sunlight? One good strategy is to identify *early-warning signals that tip us off when our minds are closing*. We tend to throw up a shield when we encounter an idea or an experience that might make us reshape our opinions. We can learn to feel ourselves slamming the door against possible new truth, by discovering specific cues that show us this is happening. These cues are usually subtle. We won't see purple neon lights that flash: **WARNING! THREATENING DATA! DANGER OF MIND-EXPANSION.** But with practice, subtle cues become more obvious.

✎ If you want to be open to helpful but unsettling insights, develop the habit of noticing how you feel inside when you encounter something that challenges your viewpoint. What do you experience when your mind is "threatened with expansion?" What warning signals occur when you are blocking out a good idea that might disturb preconceptions? For example, is an alarm going off in your mind right this minute, as you think about learning to notice the times when your mind is closing? If you can identify cues that alert you when this is happening, you can learn to catch your own mind-gate just as it starts to swing shut.

Some cues are felt in the body and others are more "mental." You may feel a vague unease, or an urge to find some rationalization that will defang the threatening datum. Perhaps you will sense a mild irritation or a sudden desire to focus on something else. Do you tighten your jaw? Do you repeat your own arguments more emphatically, either silently or out loud? Do you feel like backing away, turning away, or running away? What can tip you off that you are keeping your mind-box closed?

Personally, I tend to hold my breath and focus on counter-arguments. I may not even state these arguments aloud, but by concocting a rebuttal that I find cogent and clever, I feel relieved. I have succeeded once again in fending off the threat of mind-expansion.

Every time you read more of this book you can watch for moments when you encounter something plausible but disturbing. When that happens, check what you're feeling inside. Once you know what happens when you are threatened with expansion, be on the lookout for that cue when you're with people who challenge your belief system.

One fellow gave me a candid example of the conscious avoidance of unsettling ideas: "I met a woman at the park where I go for my daily 'constitutional,' and subsequently met her a few times more for 'walkies' . . . On one occasion, she directed me to a couple of vids on YouTube purporting to be miraculous healings. I found them disturbing, because they confront me with the question, what if, despite all reason and all other evidence, there really is a God of the biblical sort? It is too monstrous to bear much contemplation. The implication is that we are all subject – for eternity! – to the whims of a cruel and capricious power beyond all understanding, let alone control . . . My reaction is to look away, because I don't believe I have the knowledge necessary to refute their miraculous status. It helps to think about fabulous illusions of magicians, which are miraculous until you see how they're done. I have come to avoid the lady, because I cannot feel easy when threatened with miracles."

Now here is another way to practice open-mindedness. This one stirred up some resistance in those who read early drafts of *Bridging the God Gap.* (As I mentioned, all exercises are optional, but I do suggest trying out the ones that seem challenging.)

> ✎ *My Bias Inventory.* Try listing at least five of your own biases about religious issues. (Does that sound appealing or unpleasant? What mental or behavioral cues show that you are feeling enthusiastic or defensive?) What are you *emotionally inclined* to believe, so that it would be hard to make a factual case that convinced you otherwise? I've made such a list, but I suggest you write your own before reading mine.

If you tried this, what was it like? Was it easy or difficult? Was your list long or short? Try identifying the two items on your list that seem the most questionable. (For my list, see this endnote.)[47]

A Gospel of Ignorance

I think most people are grossly overconfident about their own knowledge. People who have trouble balancing their checkbooks think they know how to fix the economy. Folks who can't cope with irritable spouses figure that if they were President they could make peace in the Middle East. And even very well-informed individuals disagree about religion, psychology, psychotherapy, child rearing, education, nutrition, medicine, economics, and criminal justice.

> ❖ **Whenever large numbers of sincere and competent people *persistently* disagree, we probably do not know who is right.**

We can sometimes know the truth about controversial issues even though competent people disagree, but in general, whenever large numbers of good-hearted, well-informed, mentally-competent individuals persistently disagree, it is difficult to know whether anyone is correct. And so, we are ignorant.

I deliberately chose the blunt word "ignorant" rather than something softer, such as imperfect or fallible. Some readers have found this harsh word disturbing, but it did get their attention. We don't know nearly as much as we think we do.

We do not even know enough to understand the extent of our own ignorance. How strange that there is something instead of nothing! How bizarre that time slows down or speeds up when one's velocity changes. Astrophysicists now speculate that 95 percent of what makes up the universe is "dark matter," which we are only beginning to investigate.[48] Thomas Edison was hardly exaggerating when he said, "We don't know one millionth of one percent about anything."

In matters of religion our ignorance is vast. Throughout history spiritual seekers have made amazing mistakes in thinking about theology. (Just think of all the peculiar ideas defended by people who disagree with you.) And yet frankly it seems unsurprising that our fallible human minds might fail to comprehend ultimate reality. We may be trying to know the unknowable.

I have been keenly aware of my own ignorance for decades, and yet I still find myself imagining that my picture of reality is mostly correct. I just need to tie up a few loose ends. It's more accurate to think of my world-view as a 1% completed jigsaw puzzle. One of my early talks on this subject was called "A Gospel of Ignorance." Gospel means good news, and in my book *Do Think Twice* I have suggested that admitting ignorance is actually positive and empowering. I appreciate James P. Carse's notion of a *higher ignorance,* a state of admitted unknowing that "is the beginning of wisdom." "The more we are aware of the limitations of our knowledge, the more awake we are to the world's enormous varieties."[49]

We can reduce our own ignorance by immersing ourselves in some particular subject, but we can't do that for every field of study. Have you spent years studying theology? Do you plan to? Few will take up such a time-consuming task, and why should they? We don't all need to be religious scholars. Many will be content to say, "My personal convictions seem to fit the facts fairly well, and that's good enough for me." But if we believe or disbelieve in God without deeply exploring this issue, shouldn't we respect other people's theological views instead of dogmatically dismissing them?

Admitting ignorance tends to make people more agnostic about philosophical, religious, moral, and political matters. Here then is a radial outline which is sketched from an agnostic's perspective:

From an agnostic:

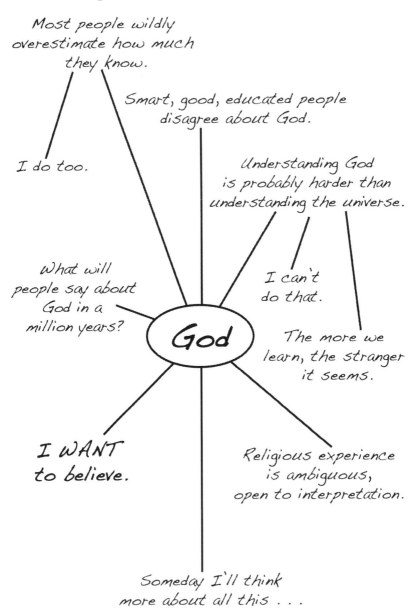

Most people wildly overestimate how much they know.

I do too.

Smart, good, educated people disagree about God.

Understanding God is probably harder than understanding the universe.

What will people say about God in a million years?

I can't do that.

God

The more we learn, the stranger it seems.

I WANT to believe.

Religious experience is ambiguous, open to interpretation.

Someday I'll think more about all this . . .

One way to cope with our own radical ignorance is to become more open to seemingly contradictory ideas. For the rest of the chapter we will explore this possibility.

The Power of Paradox

Because life is so mysterious and we know so little, it sometimes seems as if two opposite ideas are equally true. Consider these pairs of dueling proverbs:

Birds of a feather flock together, but *opposites attract.*
You're never too old to learn, but *you can't teach an old dog new tricks.*
He [or she] who hesitates is lost, but *look before you leap.*
If at first you don't succeed, try, try again, but *don't beat a dead horse.*
Lie down with dogs, get up with fleas, but *if you can't lick 'em, join 'em.*
The early bird gets the worm, but (as Steven Wright points out) *the second mouse gets the cheese.*

Isn't it remarkable how frequently some time-tested proverb contradicts another aphorism that seems just as compelling? It's often true that those who hesitate are lost, but it's also important to look before leaping. Each proverb is helpful in some situations and misleading in others. It's best to keep both principles in mind, even though they seem to collide with each other.

If we closely examine our own thoughts we may be surprised to discover contradictory inclinations. According to George Lakoff, research has shown that our conceptual systems "are not internally consistent. It is normal for people to operate with multiple models in various domains. Thus, one may have a number of inconsistent models of what a marriage should be like or how a computer works."[50]

I have come to the conclusion that it's sometimes best to openly accept two seemingly opposite beliefs. Saying this feels risky, but as Ralph Waldo Emerson remarked, "A foolish consistency is the hobgoblin of little minds, adored by little statesmen and philosophers and divines." (By the way, I am not citing page numbers for brief quotations, such as this one, that are readily available on line.)

"G. K. Chesterton comments that sanity consists in not worrying over much about consistency – that ordinary persons tend to stay sane because they care more for truth than they do for consistency." So writes the Rev. Bruce Bode. "Ordinary persons, if they see two truths that seem to contradict each other, take the truths and the contradiction with them . . . . Their sight is stereoscopic, binocular. They see two different pictures at once and are healthier and larger for it." We have "the greatest feeling of error with the most consistent systems because such systems have reduced themselves in size in order to achieve consistency. . . . They have chosen to be airtight, and, thus, suffer from a lack of air."[51]

Bode contends that, "With respect to an image of God, we can be theist, deist, polytheist, pantheist, atheist, and agnostic all at once. There can be something in each perspective that speaks to us and carries a truth for us. At one time we may lean more in one direction, and at another time in another . . . . A principle of complementary perspectives, and a willingness to live with paradox and even flat-out contradiction, can help to keep us alive and open to this beautiful, terrible world in which we live."[52]

It is our own inner multiplicity which allows us to change and grow. Unless some part of my mind dares to challenge my current beliefs, those beliefs will relentlessly persist. On the other hand, accepting paradox is not an excuse to be lazy. We should iron out as many inconsistencies as we can, and I assume that if we had perfect knowledge we would see through all apparent contradictions. Since we do not, we are often pulled in two opposite directions. As long as we realize what we're doing, we can admit that two contrary ways of thinking may both seem correct.

Think about the age-old controversy about free will. Do we freely make our own choices, at least some of the time? It seems as if we do, and yet it also seems as if every action is part of a lawful chain of causes and effects.

In a previous book I have spelled out my own solution to this puzzle in excruciating detail,[53] but I recognize that thinking about free will can be extremely confusing. For those who don't want to stumble through a maze full of philosophical bear-traps, the best strategy may be to boldly embrace the contradiction: "My decisions both are and are not freely chosen. In specific situations I can often sense which side of this paradox is correct, but sometimes I'm not sure about that. Perhaps in time I will learn more about when and in what ways I am truly free, and how I can expand the scope of my freedom."

Living with Contradictions

Embracing paradox can be useful, but one cannot always act on both sides of a contradiction at once. Should you look before you leap? Perhaps, but you cannot stand on the diving board and plunge off at the same time. How can we know when to apply one principle and when to apply another? I have no easy answers, but here is a suggestion which has been helpful to me and to some of my parishioners in dealing with theology. See if you might like to try this approach:

> ✎ *The split-level strategy.* Part of me can affirm one side of a contradiction while another part accepts the other side. That way I can think and feel in two opposite ways at almost the same time – mental multi-tasking. To try this strategy, think of some way in which you feel ambivalent about whether there is a god or what that god is like. Reflect on one side of this ambivalence today and the other tomorrow. Do this a few times till you begin to develop an intuitive sense about when to switch perspectives. Sometimes it will feel right to affirm your faith, and other times you will feel drawn toward exploring your doubts.

I realize that some readers will limit the application of this strategy, because it might violate their own convictions. We all need to be true to our principles. With that warning in mind, I want to emphasize the following paradox:

❖ **"I'm right about religion"**
versus "I might be quite wrong."
I strongly recommend developing both attitudes.

Most of us are already equipped with a well-functioning I'm-right attitude, but the open, "floaty" state of acknowledging ignorance is harder to attain. If we admit our own ignorance we will stop thinking "my side is right and everyone else is just being willfully silly."

❖ **We can think of each**
theological position as a lookout post,
seeing the world from a particular angle.

Being open-minded does not mean abandoning your personal point of view. On the contrary, you are responsible for staffing your lookout post faithfully, accurately reporting what you see from that special vantage point. Do not put down your binoculars! We need your reports. But you can also listen to reports from other posts, and occasionally visit their platforms to see what they are observing.

Summing up: The world's most popular "religion" is the worship of our own opinions.

Whenever significant numbers of sincere and competent people persistently disagree, we probably do not know who is correct.

We can learn to notice early-warning signals that tip us off when our minds are closing.

Sometimes it is best to accept contradictory beliefs, allowing ourselves to sway back and forth between opposite inclinations.

We can think of each lifestance as a lookout post, observing the world from a single vantage point. None of us can see from every angle at once, and that's one reason we need each other.

We share fleeting lifetimes in this beautiful, bewildering world, this crazy-quilt jumble of paradox and contradiction. To move ahead more steadily we can reach out to those challenging companions whose opinions critique and balance our perspective – friends and adversaries who notice what we have missed. If we never saw through each other's eyes, we would be nearly blind.

Chapter Three
God Meets the Mind Machine

Ihave been intrigued by what might be called *neurotheology*, the use of brain science to better understand religion. Brain science is quite complex, but for our purposes there is no need to go into elaborate detail. Just a few simple principles will help us see how we form theological opinions and how we can communicate with those who disagree with us about deity. In dealing with these topics I will draw upon neuroscience, psychology, and my experiences as a pastoral counselor.

Go Play with Your Thinkertoys

The brain creates beliefs through patterns of neural activity.[54] Every time a nerve cell is activated, it sends a signal to thousands of other neurons, and these send signals to thousands more, forming an intricate pattern. I simplify this complicated idea by remembering one of my childhood playthings. I picture neural patterns as a constantly changing Tinkertoy sculpture, with billions of inter-connected spools and dowels. We could call this interconnected system our *thinkertoys*.

Theists generally say that we are more than just our brains. That may be so, but if our essence is spiritual rather than physical, one of the soul's greatest challenges is to learn how to play with its thinker-toys.

The Tinkertoy image helps me realize that my beliefs are not stored, the way we store books on a shelf. What is stored is not the belief but the *inclination* to believe, the *tendency* for a particular opinion to pop up into one's mind. Suppose someone asks whether you believe in Allah. You will quickly find yourself experiencing an opinion in response to that question. If you are asked the same question later on, your brain will probably re-activate this belief, as if it were re-assembling a familiar Tinkertoy sculpture.

Some readers may think of beliefs as more stable and enduring, and that's certainly OK. But by thinking of a belief as something I have *right this second,* when some situation triggers it, I can see more clearly that beliefs are changeable constructions, here one minute and gone the next.

I realize that some religious convictions are definite and predictable, as reliable as the way a light goes on when you flip the switch. But many opinions about religion are vague and capricious, changing from one day (or one moment) to the next. Instead of being all-or-nothing, like a light flipping on or off, a belief may be more like a smear of fingerpaint, slapped down impulsively rather than carefully thought out. Our religious opinions are not always worked out carefully, as if each of us carried around a little theology book in our heads. Instead, beliefs tend to be fragmentary and disorganized, chaotic half-thoughts rather than a tidy list of bullet-points.

Here's another key discovery, based on an enormous amount of research data.[55] Our "thinkertoys" are partially assembled by unconscious brain mechanisms. In fact, it seems to me that we know very little about the way our beliefs are put together. Most of this process happens non-consciously, hidden from awareness.

Psychologist Robert Ornstein suggests that the brain is organized into "squadrons of simpletons," legions of cellular machines toiling away inside our heads.[56] Hidden brain processors are constantly performing neurological gymnastics, figuring out how to deal with one challenge after another (a traffic jam, a crying baby, a cranky boss). The individual units are unintelligent, but working together they can be brilliant. Even so, these simpletons often stumble. For instance, the mechanisms that assemble our words can become confused, sometimes because of information-processing errors and sometimes because of our personal idiosyncrasies. Psychological quirks can trigger a Freudian slip, which has been wryly defined as "intending to say one thing but actually saying a mother."

Some people think they can observe their own mental processes quite well, including the way they form beliefs. Perhaps they are right, and perhaps I am overly skeptical about our ability to monitor our own minds. But I maintain that out of urgent necessity we are mostly unaware of the tiny mental robots that serve us 24/7. It would be dangerously distracting, for example, to know that it took 88 steps for assorted brain modules to concoct the next sentence that I type. Therefore most mental activity happens discreetly out of sight.

Our ignorance of background mental processes makes it easy to assume that our judgments about religion are perfectly sensible, but the hidden machinations of cerebral simpletons sometimes fabricate beliefs with no solid basis at all. *I doubt that any of us would regard our judgments about religion as being entirely sound, if we could see a cutaway view of the way we actually construct them.*

To see what I'm driving at, think about other people's religious views. Isn't it easy to imagine others believing things for superficial reasons? Don't they seem to be misled by clever slogans, silver-tongued teachers or preachers, stories that stir their emotions, or the urge to rebel against authority figures? Can't you imagine them rejecting traditional religion in order to feel superior, or accepting doctrines because they learned them in childhood, long before they knew how to think for themselves?

Some scientists believe "that people's gut-level reaction to issues like the death penalty, taxes and abortion" is partly predetermined by genetic patterns which are physically etched into their brains. Several studies have shown "that people's general approach to social issues – more conservative or more progressive – is influenced by genes."[57] If so, some of our religious convictions may be biologically biased, but it would be difficult for us to know that about ourselves. When asked why we are religiously liberal or conservative, few of us would say that it feels as if we were born to prefer those opinions, but perhaps that's exactly what happened.

Speaking of irrational thinking, a speech coach once told me that the impact of a public lecture depends 70% on what the speaker looks like, 25% on what he or she sounds like, and 5% on the lecture's content. Was this an exaggeration? Maybe not, considering the politicians we vote into office. In any case, his comment highlights the mindless, mechanical ways in which we often create our personal convictions.

People sometimes reconsider their own beliefs, and this re-evaluation process traces new patterns of neural connections. But this may only modestly increase the odds that their beliefs will change. Longstanding patterns of deeply ingrained neural tracings will probably continue to dominate their thoughts, feelings, and actions.

The brain's operations do not act like a financial spreadsheet, in which changes in one line automatically alter the bottom line. Etching a new brain groove may make little difference to the other grooves. That's why people may hold on to a belief even after hearing a highly persuasive critique. Altering the brain means altering a complex phys-ical structure, and attitudes will not change unless old neural patterns are superseded by new patterns.

Our confidence in our own beliefs may seem verified by feelings of certainty, but with philosophical questions there is only a loose relationship between feeling confident and being correct. Just as I take my own confidence as evidence that I am right, others may think their feelings of certainty show that I am wrong. A solid, comforting confi-dence in our own viewpoint may arise within us mechanically, with no basis other than the fact that human brains tend to produce reassuring feelings of certainty. In reality, feeling confident may only prove that . . . somebody feels confident.

Realizing that we cannot observe the unconscious aspects of opinion-formation, I have come to a conclusion that may sound startling but which is actually fairly obvious. *None of us know what we believe.*

I'm not saying people are grotesquely deluded about their own convictions, thinking they are Jews when they are actually Hindus.

But when people spend time reflecting upon what they do and don't believe, they usually make numerous discoveries, sometimes minor and sometimes quite surprising. Perhaps they have become critical of ideas they once affirmed. Perhaps some doctrine they once doubted now seems clearly correct. They didn't notice these changes until they took time out to think systematically about religious issues. In short, they did not know what they really believed.

Since our minds are often controlled by the brain's non-conscious "squadrons of simpletons," how can we respond more reflectively?

> ✎ To become less mechanical, both believers and skeptics can cultivate a strategy which we could call **the positive pause.** We have all noticed the difference between reacting reflexively and reacting after reflection, and one fine time to practice the positive pause is in ticklish talks about religion. When you start to react automatically to some comment about theology, take a couple of deep breaths and think of a more constructive response.

The first response is habit. The second response is yours. Your second response is when *you* step forward and the mind machine steps aside. It's a little moment of personal birth. If you don't have lots of second responses, you aren't showing up to live your life.

Your Many Minds

Although we may think we control our minds, like a driver steers a car, this top-down model does not fit the facts. If we could easily rule our own minds we could effortlessly eliminate destructive ways of thinking and keep our thoughts focused at will. But eliminating a habitual thought pattern can take years, and novice meditators find it hard to control their thoughts for more than a few seconds.

As it turns out, the brain is relatively decentralized. It's actually a system of systems. Since our minds are fragmented into various agencies which sometimes work at cross-purposes, we may need to rethink the common assumption that each of us is a single self. Instead we can imagine that each of us consists of various mini-minds or sub-personalities.

Here are some examples of multi-mindedness:

Max goes to the refrigerator, lifts out a wedge of pumpkin pie, and eats half of it before he notices what he's doing.

Jan writes poetry, but doesn't feel like she's the one who's writing it. "It's coming through me; it flows out of my pen."

Reggie is a regular churchgoer who encourages his friends to come to services. But when he reads about interfaith violence he sometimes thinks religion is nonsense.

The mini-mind concept is meant as a metaphor and should not be taken too literally, but it helps us understand our shifting religious attitudes. Many believers have recurring moods of skepticism, and some non-believers have sub-personalities that pray. Several of my parishioners have confided that "part of me believes in God and part of me doesn't." As the Rev. Frances West puts it, "The humanist and the theist live in me, each sometimes puzzled by the presence of the other, but willing to keep talking. So may it continue."[58]

Here's an example of how people think about religious issues in contradictory ways. David Ewing Duncan tells of an experiment in which he had to respond yes or no to various statements by using a hand-clicker. One statement was *There is a god.* Duncan sees himself as nonreligious, and he often agrees with writers such as Sam Harris and Christopher Hitchens. "And yet I lack definitive proof that God does not exist. . . . If there is even a 0.0001 percent chance that this is so, can I answer no? Time is up. My thumb moves toward yes, and I press it." On the other hand, Duncan was asked later whether God is compassionate. "I would like there to be a good God who is kind and caring . . . But I see no proof of this, so I answer no."[59]

Duncan asserted God's existence because there is *some* chance this claim is correct. But he answered no to the question about divine compassion because he saw no *proof* that God is good. These two questions acted as brain probes. Each probe tickled different sequences of neurons, activating different ways of judging truth and falsity. He responded to one statement by thinking, "If there's any chance that this is right, I'll say yes." He responded to the other statement by thinking, "I won't answer yes without solid proof." This sort of inconsistency is not at all unusual. If we carefully examine our own thoughts, virtually all of us will make similar discoveries. We rearrange our theological thinkertoys from one situation to the next.

As a psychotherapist I encountered many inconsistent opinions about theology, often unnoticed by the client. I remember Eileen, who attended an Episcopal church that emphasized divine compassion. After attending services, she usually felt calm and optimistic. It seemed as if God's spirit was with her, bathing her in a warm glow of loving acceptance. On the other hand, when she came to a counseling session feeling depressed, she feared God's judgment. Thus her sense of the divine was strongly shaped by what she was currently experiencing. Being in church gave her a lift, but being depressed triggered a very different set of attitudes about religion.

If you want to become more aware of inner contradictions, you might try the following experiment:

✎ Identify a few of your own philosophical inconsistencies. See if you can list at least five. When you think about the big questions of life, you may feel pulled in various directions. Is there a god? What is God like? What is our highest purpose? Is there life after death? Are paranormal phenomena such as predicting the future fact or fiction? Reflect on one or more of these issues and see if you can sense that part of you tends to affirm one idea and another part leans in the opposite direction.

This endnote lists some of my inner contradictions.[60]

The Neural Womb of Deity

Several authors have suggested that the brain is hard-wired for religious belief.[61] Others argue against the idea that humanity is fated to remain theistic. If we were genetically programmed to be theists we should see evidence of this in virtually all cultures, but studies show huge disparities in belief. For example, when asked whether they are atheist or agnostic about the existence of a personal god, 3 - 9% of Americans say yes, compared to 31 - 44% of the British. Such data "deliver a heavy blow to this new explanation of theism."[62]

It does seem clear, however, that the brain is wired up to make small children believe almost anything grown-ups tell them. Although some of us revise our views later on, the words of Ignatius of Loyola still ring true: "Give me a child till he is seven, and I care not who has him after."

M. D. Faber has suggested that a baby's repeated experiences of parental nurture prepare the infant for religions which worship the Great Mother or the Heavenly Father. "He makes contact easily with the supernatural domain because in a manner of speaking *he has been there all along*. He has been living with or in the company of powerful, unseen, life-sustaining presences . . . ."[63]

Different Route, Different Results

Here is a highly practical idea that is woefully under-utilized. Because the brain processes information in a wide variety of ways, we can send messages through different brain pathways to get different results.

Here's an example. Some say that in order to evaluate a religious doctrine, we must belong to a spiritual community that affirms this doctrine. Outsiders may think they understand some concept of God, for instance, but if they do not fully commit themselves to this belief through worship and private devotions, they cannot judge whether it's true or false.

The insider's experience and the outsider's experience send messages through different neural pathways, and people think and feel differently as a result. An insider's experiences may stimulate emotion, perception, mental imagery, and physical activity such as kneeling, singing hymns, and taking communion. Outsiders tend to be more detached, without as much emotion, perception, imagery, and action.

Personally, I see both approaches as useful. We can learn a lot by thinking about theology with cool-headed logic. We can learn other things by throwing ourselves into a clapping-and-stomping revival meeting. Words activate some brain patterns, meditation activates others, and music mobilizes still others. When I was considering atheism in college, I told my friends that the strongest argument for Christianity was the experience of listening to the University of Redlands Concert Choir.

We can use the principle of different route/different results to contemplate religion more fruitfully and to communicate about it in more positive ways. When you think of God, try to deliberately jingle diverse connections in your own mind/brain. You can reflect on religious issues in ways that are emotionally intense or emotionally detached, and you can seek out contrasting inputs – read both Richard Dawkins and Eric Reitan.

The rerouting principle can also make communication about religion less stressful. Positive communication sends messages through different pathways than if we conveyed the same content in a tense, aggressive, or condescending manner. Different route, different results.

Merely approaching a situation focusing on warm feelings toward another person can make a huge difference. At some level your friend will probably sense your good intent. This constructive attitude will help both of you loosen up, which will make it easier to convey messages such as:

❀ Even though we disagree, we can appreciate each other's sincerity.

❀ My criticism of your beliefs is not an indictment of your character.

You'll find more suggestions about respectful communication in Chapter Four.

Summing up: The formation of religious convictions, like all other mental processes, partly depends on the brain's squadrons of simpletons, and these mechanisms often make mistakes. If we could see an X-ray view of the way we form our own beliefs, we might be appalled.

The mind is decentralized and fragmented, functioning more like a committee than like a drill team. Members of this committee may have contradictory beliefs about theology.

There is a big difference between automatically reacting and reacting after reflection. *The first response is habit. The second response is yours.*

Chapter Four
Disarming Conversation

Many fine books are full of suggestions about effective communication.[64] In this chapter I'll just mention a few basic principles which are helpful in discussing religion. To some readers this may seem like a digression, but most of us could benefit from a brief communication tune-up.

Before reading further I invite you to tap into your own wisdom. All of us know a lot about how to address emotionally loaded topics. We just need to remember to apply what we know, in the heat of controversy. Remind yourself of what you have already discovered about helpful and unhelpful communication. If you like, make a list of what to do and what to avoid, with at least five items in each category.

Stop Before You Start?

Perhaps the first question to ask in thinking of discussing religion is whether it even makes sense to try. Sometimes mentioning a touchy subject just stirs up hurt and anger, with no realistic hope of making progress. When differences are extreme and emotions are raw, it may be best to skirt the issue altogether. You can still look for ways to build rapport through mutually enjoyable activities. And by reading this book you may learn to understand your friend in ways that help the two of you get along.

Too often, however, people give up without making any effort to communicate. It's easy to assume that other people are rigid or irrational. If in doubt, prepare for the conversation carefully, watch for the right time, and see what happens. If it doesn't work out, at least you gave it your best.

Establish realistic expectations. Instead of hoping to totally eliminate discomfort about religious differences, your goal might be to find out more about what the other person believes. As I have mentioned, people's theological opinions are often more complex than they seem on the surface.

Here are a few ways to initiate an interchange about God.

❀ Check your friend's receptivity. "I sometimes criticize your religious views, and vice versa. Maybe we should sit down some time and see if we can understand each other better. Do you think it's worth a try?"

❀ Watch for an instance of friction about religion, and then say something like: "This issue has been coming between us for a long time, hasn't it? Maybe we should talk about the whole God-thing. I'd like to find out why you believe as you do and tell you more about where I'm coming from."

❀ Show your friend this book. "Our friendship matters to me, and it makes me sad that religion creates tension between us. I've been reading a book about finding common ground in spite of theological disagreements, and I've been trying to get up my courage to broach this subject."

❀ If the person seems receptive, invite him or her to make a commitment. "I have some time tomorrow to talk about this. Would that be OK?"

Practicing Positive Communication

Here are seven strategies that help disarm difficult conversations about theology.

1. Pre-communicate. Talk about what you're going to talk about. Say what you hope to accomplish. "There's a distance between us because of our religious beliefs. I would like to take a little step toward bridging that gap." You may want to frankly acknowledge that one discussion won't fix everything. Change happens little by little.

2. Once you begin, keep your main goals in mind. Concentrate on the most important items instead of getting lost in a dust-storm

of details. State one or two central points, and repeat them so that they stand out. We are not tape recorders. We do not hear each other perfectly. Repetition is often necessary in order for people to absorb messages. Resist the temptation to veer off onto trivial tangents to make an impressive point.

3. Throughout the conversation, try to stay connected, heart to heart. Without knowing it we may approach a dialogue about religion as if we've entered a physical fight. When we smite someone on the forehead with a particularly weighty argument, we may expect this poor benighted soul to bow down in surrender, grateful for having been shown the light. How disappointing when people just resent us for making them look stupid.

Attitude is crucial. If you are sincerely interested in connecting with another human being, he or she will probably feel safe enough to open up. Even if you stumble and stammer, your good intentions will come across. But if your goal is to attack, debate, or dominate, it's hard to conceal this agenda with handy-dandy communication techniques.

When you start to lose personal connection, you might say, "I can feel myself starting to treat this like a battle. But I care about you and I want to treat you right." Be especially careful if you find yourself getting flustered. Do not blurt things out while you are upset. When I notice myself starting to sputter, that's a tip-off that I'm about to become obnoxious, inarticulate, or both. Take a breath, and remember that your goal is to reach out, not put down.

(Isn't it?)

To help stay connected, be big-hearted about criticism. Refrain from firing back impulsively, shooting from the hip. When attacked, listen and reflect before responding. After pausing to regain clarity – and charity – show your critic that you can see how it looks from his or her viewpoint, even if you don't agree. Then say what you believe.

4. Listen well, and ask to be heard in return. Think of talk radio as an example of how not to speak and listen respectfully. Be honest with yourself about your own conversational faults. Do you resort to sarcasm? Personal attacks? Name-calling? A condescending tone of voice or facial expression? If you catch yourself being hostile or demeaning you can admit it and apologize. People appreciate such candor and humility.

In listening to another person, remember inner inconsistency and multiplicity. Most of us are quite complicated and at times even self-contradictory. In each conversation, see if you can identify at least two different sets of beliefs corresponding to at least two of your friend's mini-minds. If you cannot, you are probably just in touch with surface appearances. Admittedly, only one sub-personality might manifest itself in a single interchange. That should remind us that one conversation seldom provides sufficient insight, in dealing with something as multifaceted as religious belief.

Here are a few examples of attitudes that might materialize while talking about religion:

❀ Stubborn and negative, thoroughly defended against spiritual or intellectual expansion.
❀ Bored with the whole topic, anxious to turn on the TV and ditch this discussion.
❀ Interested and curious, open to learning more.
❀ Thoughtful and analytical, wanting to solve puzzles and state problems clearly.
❀ Caring and compassionate, ready to connect in spite of obstacles.

Remember, the sub-personality concept should not be taken too literally. It's just a useful way of discovering inconsistency and multiplicity in others . . . and in ourselves.

5. Treat this talk as an opportunity to practice clear awareness. Raise your antennae, and tune in to more than the obvious. Com-

munication isn't just kicking words around like a soccer ball. We also send messages with our tone of voice, how fast or loud we are talking, and what we do *not* say. Be aware also of posture, body position, facial expressions, movements, gestures, and eye contact (or the lack of it).

Talking about religion is an exercise in empathetic imagination. We communicate best when we notice what the other person is feeling and thinking, and what we will sometimes sense is pain. People are distressed when their views about religion are questioned. When we become distressed we need to talk it out, so as to diminish the pressure we feel inside. Then we are able to think more clearly.

6. Practice meta-communication, communication about communication. Comment occasionally about how this chat is progressing. Express appreciation for what's working well. Mention ways that you are trying to be constructive and ways your friend seems to be doing the same. Be gracious about admitting glitches and commit yourself to doing better.

7. In addition to pre-communication and meta-communication, practice post-communication. After you say something important, check to see if your message was received. It has been said that the main problem with communication is *the illusion that it has been accomplished.* Don't just make noises in the direction of your friend and assume that your message is getting through. Find out what he or she is hearing. "The main thing I'm trying to say is _____ Do you see what I'm driving at?"

Conversely, make sure you are hearing clearly:

"Basically, then, you are saying _____. Is that right?"

"Are you saying ____ or are you saying ____?"

Before parting, thank your friend for sharing something personal and significant.

Few rules are absolute, and any set of guidelines can backfire under certain circumstances. Let each situation guide your actions. But these seven time-tested principles usually work just fine.

Troubleshooting

In spite of our best intentions, dialogues about religious differences may deteriorate into a verbal shoving contest. One person pushes an idea at the other, who then resists by pushing it away. We mentally tug and struggle, revving up our bodies with a brain-fogging surge of adrenalin. Important: When you push against people and they start pushing back, you are actually encouraging them to restate (and therefore strengthen) their own point of view. That is probably not your objective!

Watch out for symptoms that appear when a conversation turns into a tug-o'-war:

In yourself: Holding your breath; tightness in your jaw, neck, shoulders, or back; butterflies or burning sensations in your stomach; and feelings of frustration, exasperation, anger, or self-righteousness.

In your friend: Talking loudly or angrily; name-calling or put-downs; a frown or other facial grimace; and belligerent body language such as crossing the arms, shaking a fore-finger, or leaning forward as if to invade your territory.

If one of you starts to tense up, take time to let go of pushing and/or resisting. You may want to say something like, "I know that we both want to respect and understand each other. I don't want to force ideas down your throat. Maybe we should take a break and make some tea."

When people say things that seem wildly out of line, be sure you understand them correctly. Ask for further elaboration before you launch an attack. Even if someone says something you know is absurd, don't throw up your hands and walk away, assuming that it's impossible to reason with this numbskull. Try to be charitable. Maybe you yourself occasionally say silly things in the heat of the moment. People often make ridiculous statements in dealing with highly charged subjects, or they parrot half-baked ideas from lectures, sermons, or the Internet. Please, please realize that these debating points may have absolutely nothing to do with their real reasons for belief or disbelief. Be patient. Probe further. And try to draw out your own deepest reasons, instead of just tossing sharp barbs you hope will stick.

What to avoid:

Don't assume that the other person has inferior motives and values.

Don't look down on others from a smugly superior position.

Don't interrupt, but do get your ideas out.

Don't overgeneralize. Always remember never to say *always* and *never*.

Don't shout, "How can you think such a thing?" (unless you want to advertise the limits of your own understanding).

Be careful about offering suggestions. These may be taken as criticisms and as attempts to control. Repeated suggestions will be seen as nagging.

Let's consider some specific cases of communication about religion. Here's a communication snafu mentioned on a secular humanist website called sweetreason.org:

Dear Sweet Reason,

My middle son is a devout Evangelical Christian. When I visit him we often go for a walk at a state park near his house that displays fossils. I use that as an opportunity to start a conversation about science and creationism, but he gets sullen and clams up. I want to try to open his mind a bit, but apparently I'm going about it the wrong way. Can you suggest anything?

– Evolving with Increasing Perplexity

Dear Perplexed,

Unless your son is at risk of doing something dangerous, just back off, at least for now . . . [F]ind ways you can enjoy each other's company and interests; . . . whatever is needed to show respect for his independence, and build affection and trust. Bear in mind that if your son is going to respond to intellectual arguments (the approach you've been trying), he might not do so when the arguments come from his father, of all people. . . . Meanwhile, try to understand why he is devout. Anyone's beliefs (yours and mine, too) can be understood as a result of the influence of others, and as an attempt to solve life's problems.[65]

Excellent advice. And it's good that Perplexed noticed his son's non-verbal cues. They weren't especially subtle, but people do miss the obvious. He was also wise to ask for feedback from someone outside the situation. Sweet Reason suggested focusing on the positive, building connections and rapport, and facing the fact that a father may not be in a good position to change the mind of his son.

Here's a quick workout about communication on religious issues. Imagine you are in a conversation about theology and your friend says something that makes you uncomfortable. Think about ways that you might respond. I'll give you three hot-potato examples. After each example I have suggested possible responses.

1. You are a Christian, and an atheist family member compares God to Santa Claus. How do you respond?

❏ That's an insult! How dare you mock my religion?
❏ (Grit your teeth and remain silent.)
❏ I'm not sure what you are getting at here. Do you mean that God sounds too good to be true?

2. You are an atheist, and your mother says she cries every night because you are going to hell.

❏ Oh Jesus Christ! Do we have to go through this sob story again?
❏ Mom, don't be silly. There isn't any hell.
❏ You do love me so much, Mom. I hate to see you feeling bad.

3. You are an agnostic and a friend says, "How can you look at this incredible sunset and doubt that God is real?"

❏ And how can you look at all the suffering in this world and be so certain that God's in charge?
❏ Thanks for pointing out this amazing sunset. I love nature too, even though I'm not convinced that a divine being makes it beautiful. Can you understand how I could feel that way?
❏ How about them Yankees?

The actual meaning of hot-potato comments 1, 2, and 3 might vary, depending on factors such as context, tone of voice, etc. But I'm sure you can see the advantages of the third answer to 1 and 2, and the second answer to 3.

Evocative Questions and Other Techniques

In learning what a friend or family member believes, asking open-ended, evocative questions can be helpful. Instead of posing a yes/no query such as, "Do you believe in God?" try, "What are your thoughts about God?" Evocative statements are sometimes even better than questions, because questions can make people feel as if they are being interrogated. To a theist one could say: "I would appreciate knowing more about how you see religion. Maybe you

could tell me about your understanding of God, what God is like."
It is also helpful to draw out the experiential basis of belief or
disbelief. To an atheist one could say: "I'm interested in what has
led you to say there is no God. Can you tell me a little about that?"
You can also offer to discuss what has led you to your own lifestance.

Other evocative questions:

❀ What first inclined you toward the beliefs you have today? Did
you accept them when you were a child? When you had grown up?
❀ What have you found helpful in your beliefs? What makes you
feel good? What other benefits do you receive?
❀ Today, what do you *most* appreciate about your faith tradition
or philosophy of life?
❀ How does your faith tradition or philosophy of life help make
this a better world?

✎ *Role reversal.* This is a communication technique from relationship counseling. Do a little play-acting and imagine yourselves agreeing with each other's point of view. Or you can do
this by yourself, acting out both sides.

You may want to:
1. Talk about what it would feel like to believe this way.
2. Say what could lead a person to accept the position you are
taking in the role-play.
3. Identify what you see as the greatest strength of this position.

I'll illustrate with an example: David is Jewish and believes in
God. Sandra is an agnostic. They prepare by listing a few ideas
about what it would be like to have the other person's viewpoint.
Then Jewish David begins, pretending that he is an agnostic:

"Does God exist? That involves all sorts of complicated issues.
What is ultimate reality? Is there a supernatural world? How is that

related to the world of subatomic particles that science studies? Did the Big Bang happen due to some intelligent process that occurred 'before' the beginning of time? Our minds are too small to grasp all of that. Even our most sophisticated theories about God may be full of holes. So I have no idea whether God really exists."

Agnostic Sandra then pretends to be a believer:

"Look, David, most people do believe in God, regardless of whether they're smart or stupid, Ph.D.'s or illiterates. Sure, some churches say ridiculous things about God, because they rely on stuff that was written thousands of years ago. But many people today have much more sophisticated theologies. If I had to place a bet on whether God exists, I could see good reasons to answer yes."

After the role play, they talk about what it was like. "It was easy to argue for agnosticism," says David, "since I think life is stranger than we can possibly understand. The greatest strength of agnosticism is that it focuses on the limits of our knowledge. But it would feel weird to live with such vagueness, floating along with nothing solid to stand on."

"I found it hard to support a strong belief in theism," Sandra remarks. "But I think I did a decent job of making a case for some force or entity that is way beyond our understanding, something that could be called God. One strength of theism is that there are so many possibilities about what God could be. Maybe one of them is true. I might accept God based on scientific evidence of an intelligence behind the universe, but I prefer to leave such vast matters open."

Role-playing is difficult, but it's a great way to stretch one's mind and heart, learning to see life in unfamiliar ways.

Here are two more disciplines that are challenging but helpful.

✎ *Look back and learn more.* After a conversation is over, try replaying it in your own mind to see what you can learn. I don't mean mentally revising what you said so that every sentence is devastating and you come out on top. Instead, think about ways that both you and your friend were positive and helpful. Then recall ways that you were less than constructive.

✎ *Restate, then reply.* Suppose Alice and Bob are talking and Alice speaks first. Bob will then restate the gist of Alice's message, and Alice will say whether Bob got it right. *Bob cannot reply to Alice until he restates her message to Alice's satisfaction.* Then when Bob replies, Alice summarizes his message till her restatement meets with Bob's approval, and so on. Try this for some specified amount of time, perhaps 20 minutes. The exercise may sound daunting, but it can be enjoyable if you have a sense of humor about the follies and foibles of human communication.

While reviewing the conversation, don't put yourself down. Give yourself credit for candidly assessing your own mistakes. If you pray, pray for guidance about areas of difficulty. If you do not pray, focus on your commitment to speak and listen in useful ways.

You may also wish to reflect upon questions such as these:

– What was the general tone of this dialogue?
  – Comfortable? Uncomfortable?
  – Deep? Superficial?
  – Did it seem like a sharing or a boxing match?
– What were we feeling? (Anger, fear, sadness, frustration, curiosity, empathy, hope, surprise?)
  – Toward each other?
  – About the subject?

– What did each of us respond to most positively?
  – Facts?
  – Feelings?
  – Images and analogies?
  – Anecdotes and stories?
– What else can I learn from this discussion?

Some of my suggestions will fit your personal style and some will not, but I hope you have spotted at least one or two helpful ideas. By practicing the art of disarming conversation, we are helping to change the world from a combat zone into a community of thoughtful dialogue. We are doing our part to realize the vision of Isaiah, Chapter One: "Come now, let us reason together."

Committed Relationships

(If this topic is not important to you, you may want to skim or skip ahead to the chapter summary.)

Many committed couples disagree about God, and unless they discussed theology when they were first dating, this conflict may have caught them by surprise. When spiritual issues do surface they can be painful and distressing. "'We've been going out for eight months," one woman reported, "and we get along great most of the time. The problem is that every now and then he says something like 'How could you really believe all that stuff about Jesus being the Messiah' and we get into an argument. . . . he makes fun of me like I'm some sort of idiot.'"[66]

If a couple argues repeatedly about God, the first step may be to identify specific changes that would alleviate this conflict. Here are seven possible objectives, in increasing order of difficulty:

Stop fighting dirty. No putdowns or name-calling.
Shorten the duration of arguments about religion.
Learn about what each partner believes and why.

Begin to appreciate the merits of each other's viewpoint.

Develop a sense of humor about religious disagreements.

Achieve genuine respect for the other person's lifestance.

Enjoy participating in each other's religious/non-religious communities.

The couple may also discuss how to deal with in-laws who disapprove of one partner's religious views.

Theists and atheists in committed relationships can learn from the experience of interfaith couples. For many wise and practical suggestions based on such relationships, see Rabbi Steven Carr Reuben's excellent book, *A Nonjudgmental Guide to Interfaith Marriage*. Reuben advocates a team marriage approach, in which the two partners actively cooperate in fostering religious tolerance and appreciation.

Interestingly, after countless counseling sessions with interfaith couples Reuben has concluded that "most of the time theology is *not* the real issue."[67] Instead, religion is a convenient and familiar focus for disagreement. It may be easier to quarrel about God and the Bible than to address other sensitive topics.

During conversations about religion, remember that expressing anger can make people frightened and defensive. "I felt sad when you criticized my faith" is generally less threatening than "I'm mad at you for criticizing my faith." The first statement implies vulnerability, while the second statement may sound like a snarl. Showing vulnerability often deepens intimacy. "Make a personal statement about how you *feel*," Reuben suggests: "All of a sudden I felt frightened and scared. I feel like I'm out of touch with the most important thing in my life, which is you and our relationship."[68]

A relationship is like a dance, and good dancers avoid stomping on their partners' toes. But we can't always tell when we have trampled on someone's feelings. If the two partners are relatively secure, they can agree to let the other person know when a statement hurts. They can say, "that was an Ouch," or "that stung a little." Ask each other what words or phrases will make it easier to hear this sort of feedback.

Over the course of a long-term relationship, a couple can practice positive communication techniques so they become second nature. Living with someone also makes it easier to notice transitions from one sub-personality to another. If a closed-minded sub-self is in control, discussing God would be a waste of time. But later a curious and thoughtful mini-mind may emerge, opening the door to meaningful exploration.

In addition to noticing sub-personalities, we can also tune in to a sort of supra-personality, the relationship as a whole. Relationship counselors commonly focus on both the individual psychology of each partner and on an invisible third person, the patterns of interaction between the two partners. Michael Dowd and Connie Barlow have actually given this larger couple-self a name: "*Jasmine* is the name we use to speak of our relationship as a couple – the whole that is more than the sum of two of us. Naming our marital bond has helped us prevent minor disagreements from morphing into major ones. 'I know what you want,' I may say to Connie, 'and I know what I want, but what does Jasmine want?'"[69]

A Nonjudgmental Guide to Interfaith Marriage suggests dealing with topics such as:

"1. How to treat the holidays of the other?

2. How to raise the children, what religion will they be, and why choose that one over the other?

3. What happens to the religious training if there is a separation or divorce? . . .

4. How do you communicate . . . with your in-laws and future relatives?"[70]

In considering items 2 and 3, ask yourself, "How would you feel if you heard your children telling someone that they were the religion of your spouse?"[71]

Reuben also suggests using a sentence-completion technique:

"1. When I think of my religion . . .
2. When I don't celebrate a holiday, I feel . . .
3. As a child, religion to me was . . .
4. My favorite religious experience was . . .
5. The thing that makes me most uncomfortable about my boy/girlfriend's religion is . . .
6. The thing I like least about my own religion is . . ."[72]

Free association is another excellent exercise. Think of a religious term and notice the first words that pop into mind. This helps uncover "stereotypes, which are a normal but usually unacknowledged part of every interfaith relationship . . . For example, when I said 'cross,' Jim said 'Jesus' and Susan said 'killing.'"[73]

Dealing with the spiritual life of children is particularly tricky. Above all, "Don't create a family life that places your children in a no-win contest for religious loyalty between the religions of their mother and father."[74] Think about what you want your children to believe about *theology* and about *values*. You may find that the core values they live by are more important to you than whatever theory of the universe they eventually embrace. Fortunately there is probably a lot of overlap between your values and that of your life partner. In fact, the values of a Christian and an atheist are sometimes more compatible than the values of two Christians or two unbelievers. One Christian, for example, might be racially prejudiced while the other works for racial justice.

Reuben concludes that "What your child needs above all . . . is your unconditional love."[75] If a home is full of love, differences in lifestance may become insignificant.

Summing up: Before talking with someone about religion, decide whether there is any hope of a positive outcome. Then think about the best way to bring up the subject.

Practice pre-communication, meta-communication, and post-communication.

Try to stay connected, heart to heart. Listen well, and ask to be heard in return. Be aware of subtleties such as body language. Draw out the other person with evocative questions and statements. Consider using disciplines such as role reversal and restate-before-replying.

So far you have been invited to reflect upon:

- ❀ our love of being right
- ❀ how little we know about ultimate reality
- ❀ how brain machinery helps shape our beliefs
- ❀ how to discuss religion with clarity and respect

With this background in mind we can explore two different ways of bridging the great God gap. We can appreciate each other despite our differences, and we can discover that our beliefs have more in common than we thought.

THE BRIDGE

Chapters Five, Six, and Seven

Human Kinship
Looking Past Labels and Slogans
Mystery and Metaphor

Chapter Five
Human Kinship

"Love is the drive towards the unity of the separated."[76]
– Paul Tillich

One of my Mormon relatives put it simply: "We are all much more alike than we are different." After a conversation with conservative Christians, an atheist used almost exactly the same words: "We have much more in common than we have that separates us."

In focusing on what we have in common, I invite you to treat this chapter as a series of meditations – gentle reminders of what you already know, ideas that are simple and powerful but easily forgotten. I have included several exercises. Choose the ones that interest you, and take as much time with them as you need.

Let's begin with the most basic connection of all: We share a common humanity. It is so easy to ignore this fundamental fact. *We are all in this life together. We all breathe and bleed, love and hate, rejoice and fall into despair. We are all immersed in the human condition, small and fragile creatures in a huge and strange cosmos. And all of us undergo intense experiences of love, joy, beauty, discovery, and wonder.*

Most religions teach that humans share the same origin, the same nature, the same flaws, the same worth, and the same potential. Similarly, science teaches that we are linked by our biological ancestry. If we can remember these profound similarities, doctrinal differences may seem trivial.

David Spangler listed several aspects of our shared humanity in his book, *Blessing*:

"We want life to be our ally: helping us, empowering us, enabling us to be safe and happy. We want good things to come our way: our wounds healed, our loneliness banished, our power restored, our fears allayed. We want alienation to be replaced with belonging, impoverishment with abundance, bondage with liberation, and darkness with light.

"We want to be blessed. And in our better moments, we want to be a blessing for others."[77]

Companions in Gratitude

Gratitude is a nearly-universal value. Giving thanks to God is central in Christianity and most other faiths. Carl Sagan, a secular humanist, said that gratitude combines "elation and humility" in a way that "is surely spiritual."[78]

Many believers and non-believers can agree that *life's richest blessings are abundantly available.* We often overlook these gifts, seeing our glass as half-empty (and dreadfully water-spotted at that). But forces that move us toward healing, renewal, and fulfillment are not rare or exotic. They are available to virtually everyone whose basic needs have been met. Once we are secure in having healthful food, close friends, a comfortable place to sleep, and good care when we are sick, an overflowing cornucopia of opportunities is ours to enjoy, just by being alive.

We All Know Heartache

By the time we reach midlife nearly all of us have suffered deeply and repeatedly. Some have felt the ache of seeing love wither. Most have lost dear ones to death. We may have faced financial losses, setbacks at work, or serious health concerns. We may have done things that made us ashamed. And to the extent that we feel part of the human journey, the burdens of humanity weigh upon our shoulders.

Helen Keller's insightful comments about grief also pertain to other kinds of suffering:

"We bereaved are not alone. We belong to the largest company in the world, the company of those that have known suffering. When it seems that our sorrow is too great to be borne, let us think of the great family of the heavy hearted into which our grief has given us entrance and inevitably, we will feel about us their arms, their sympathy, their understanding."[79] "Believe, when you are most unhappy, there is something for you to do in the world. So long as you can sweeten another's pain, life is not in vain."[80]

When one of your relationships becomes strained by religious differences, reflecting upon difficulties the other person has experienced may help you feel closer. Often the burdens borne by others are part of what makes them prickly, defensive, or stubborn.

"Negative" Connections

Paradoxically, people who disagree about religion may be connected by negative factors such as their own weaknesses. For example, two people who quarrel about theology may each have unrealistic confidence in their own judgments: "I am obviously correct, and anyone who disagrees with me is either malicious or confused." Someone who seems like our opposite may actually be our mirror image. So when a theist and an atheist shout, "Go to Hell!" at each other, the main difference may be that the atheist is cursing but the theist is suggesting a literal destination!

✎ Bring to mind a person with whom you argue about some topic such as religion. Make a list of *at least 25 ways you are similar.* If you get stuck, write down trivialities: "We both love lemon meringue pie." Then keep writing. Look back at your list and see how your feelings toward that person have changed.

> ✎ *That's me.* When you are around someone who disagrees with you about God, pay attention to this individual and *imagine that he or she is you.* Does he look tired? You can picture yourself with the same weary expression. Is she drinking tea? Imagine you are the one lifting the cup to your lips.

So many things we do are virtually universal human activities – working, eating, sleeping, frowning, laughing, loving, and so on. That's one reason we are more alike than different.

So many things we do are virtually universal human activities – working, eating, sleeping, frowning, laughing, loving, and so on. That's one reason we are more alike than different.

Kindred Ignorance

The fact that we know so little is another human universal. Believers and unbelievers can be united in humility, admitting their own deep ignorance. That's why I emphasized this theme so early in the book.

Admitting the limits of my own understanding has a spiritual resonance, partly because fully facing ignorance fills me with awe. I sense this with special intensity when I go for a walk late at night. Have you ever felt this amazement, gazing at the darkened sky? How humbling to look toward the heavens – vast, unimaginable spaces surrounding our planet, filled with billions of galaxies. At times I am *seized* by the stunning realization that I have no idea what is out there, or even out there in universes beyond this one. I am struck dumb by the limitlessness of what I do not know.

As Rudolf Otto suggested in *The Idea of the Holy,* the experience of awe is at the core of religious awareness. Throughout history people have felt what Otto calls the *mysterium tremendum,* a mystery so profound that it can make us tremble. He says we encounter this *mysterium* with particular intensity in silence, in darkness, and when gazing out at vast open spaces.[81] These are the very times when I most vividly sense my own radical ignorance.

There can be a close kinship between the experience of cosmic ignorance and the feeling of wonder which accompanies religious faith. In some cases a believer, contemplating a supreme being, and a skeptic, looking with amazement at the limitless sky, may be in similar states of mind. One says, "The glory of the Lord!" The other exclaims, "What glorious galaxies!" Both are attuned to something thrilling and astonishing, something they can reach toward even though they cannot touch it.

Shared Goals and Values

Since so many theists, atheists, and agnostics want to make this a better world, we can find common ground in shared objectives. This strategy has worked wonderfully in multi-religious organizations, with people from all sorts of faith traditions pulling together to promote justice and help those in need.

In recent years I have often attended the Tri-Cities Interfaith Council Thanksgiving Service in Fremont, California which includes Christians, Jews, Muslims, Sikhs, Buddhists, Hindus, Baha'is, Mormons, Unificationists, Unitarian Universalists, and Native Americans. Their prayers, chants, and rituals are widely varied, but every presentation expresses a deeply moving sincerity. I may be uncomfortable with certain theologies or practices, but I fully respect their commitment to trying to do what's right.

Here are four ways to focus on common values with friends and family members:

❀ Talk with each other about the ideal life. Dream up creative but realistic scenarios for personal fulfillment. If you care about the larger human venture, include ways of making a difference in the wider world. What is your vision of the best possible way (or ways) to be human? How would you earn your living? How would you help others? How would you spend leisure time? What would be your greatest satisfactions?

❀ Brainstorm together about the ideal society. If you ruled the planet, what changes would you make? (Caution: If you and your friend disagree about politics this exercise might backfire.)

❀ Discuss what you have each done for the larger world and what you could do in the future. Be as specific as possible. If you want to help children, how might that goal be realized? Would you join some organization like Camp Fire USA or a local tutoring program? Would you take classes to learn helpful skills?

❀ Consider participating jointly in some project. Help clean up a local park or renovate the home of someone with physical disabilities. Enter a walk-a-thon that raises funds to cure some cruel illness. These activities forge connections that make it easier to respect each other despite theological differences.

Caring and Compassion

In *A History of God*, Karen Armstrong shows that virtually all spiritual communities emphasize compassion.[82] "The beginning and end of Torah is performing acts of loving kindness," according to the Talmud.[83] The Gospel of John shows Jesus asking Simon Peter three times, "Do you love me?" Each time Peter said yes, Jesus challenged him to *show* that love by caring for "my sheep," i.e., those who are in need (John 21:15-17). Islam teaches that faithful Muslims must give generously to "the orphans, and the needy, and the wayfarer . . . ."[84]

Many secular humanists also emphasize compassion, and unbelievers are among the best-known humanitarians. Harvard chaplain Greg Epstein points out that many twentieth-century visionaries and activists have been humanists: ". . . Abraham Maslow, Carl Rogers, Ted Turner, Isaac Asimov, Alice Walker, Kurt Vonnegut, John Kenneth Galbraith, Carl Sagan, and Betty Friedan, to name only a few."[85] I also recall what novelist Aldous Huxley said when he was nearing death: "It's a bit embarrassing to have been concerned with the human problem all one's life and find at the end that one has no more to offer than: Try to be a little kinder."[86]

The Rev. Tony Larsen offered a challenge to his congregation about strengthening kindly feelings:

"I have a homework assignment for you today. Everyone you meet today – whether it's people you know well, or strangers – I'd like you to imagine that you can see two things inside them. The two things that are inside every person are *a bright light and a wound.* Everyone has a bright light inside them – a goodness, a brightness. And everyone also has a wound, which sometimes keeps them from shining as brightly as they otherwise might. It may be a physical wound, like cancer or AIDS; it may be something more invisible, like abuse or neglect, or a desperate need for continual attention because they never got quite the affirmation they needed as a child.

"But when they do something annoying, remember that they really have a light inside. It's just their wound which keeps it from shining clearly.

"Now this doesn't mean you shouldn't *say* anything about people's annoying behavior – they may need to hear it, and maybe you should confront them. But if you remember their light *and* their wound – you will confront them [with caring].

"And remember also that *you* have a light . . . and a wound."[87]

✎ You can challenge yourself the way Tony challenged his congregation. Think of someone you love. Close your eyes and imagine him or her radiating bright light. What personal qualities shine through in that glow? Then remember that this person is in some way wounded. All of us bear scars. Can you sense where it hurts?

Now try moving up one level of difficulty. Think of someone whose religious convictions clash with your own. Hold that person in your thoughts to sense and appreciate his or her light. Then focus on this person's woundedness. See how your feelings change.

This meditation can be quite poignant in reflecting upon family members. It is especially moving to sense the brilliance and the brokenness of our own children. Perhaps personal tensions have covered up some of our caring – but the caring is still there.

✎ *Radial Outline: Our Common Humanity.* If you like, reflect on what you have in common with those whose views of religion clash with your own. Make a radial outline with "Human Kinship" in the center. List ideas about our common humanity in a circle around the page. I've included an example.

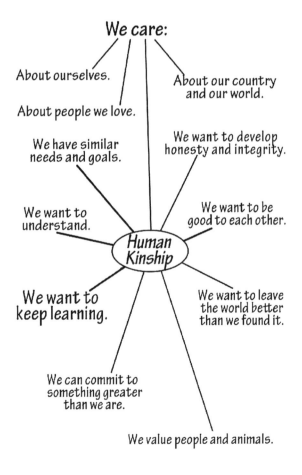

We care:

About ourselves.

About our country and our world.

About people we love.

We have similar needs and goals.

We want to develop honesty and integrity.

We want to understand.

We want to be good to each other.

Human Kinship

We want to keep learning.

We want to leave the world better than we found it.

We can commit to something greater than we are.

We value people and animals.

Out of the many things we have in common, which seem most important to you? Which commonalities help you feel close to others?

You may want to glance back through this chapter, thinking of it once again as a series of meditations. Perhaps you will decide to regularly reflect on one or two passages. Every morning I ritually remind myself that "This is a day to experience my unity with the web of all living things." We all need ways of remembering our common kinship.

Summing up: Both believers and non-believers can be grateful for life's gifts. They can also empathize with each other's burdens and sorrows.

Those who disagree about religion may have certain weaknesses in common. "Opposites" are often mirror images.

Believers and unbelievers can be united in humility, admitting the limits of their knowledge.

Most theists, atheists, and agnostics care about other people and the larger human venture.

Chapter Six
Looking Past Labels and Slogans

We have now laid the groundwork for considering a surprising possibility: Perhaps some forms of theism and atheism are far more compatible than they seem, and in some cases virtually identical. During the next two chapters I will show that the world-views of theists and atheists are often remarkably similar. It's as if they are brothers and sisters who do not recognize each other – "siblings in disguise."

Please be assured that I am not trying to deny the differences between belief systems. I won't try to show atheists and agnostics that they really believe in God without knowing it, or prove that most theists are closet skeptics. Some differences in lifestance are basic and significant. But if we can uncover partial parallels between seemingly incompatible perspectives, it will be easier to understand, communicate, and live together in peace.

Caution: Words at Play

In dealing with beliefs we need to say clearly what we mean, and that isn't easy in speaking of God. People often assume that God is the great creator described in the Bible. Yet there are several understandings of God in Scripture and a myriad of god-concepts in theology books. It's not, "Does God exist?" It's, "Which god or godlike entity exists, if any?" There are many possible gods, spirits, and esoteric energies.

"God" is what I call an octopus word. Its many definitions reach in many directions, like the waving arms of an octopus. When people argue about whether there is a god, they may be holding different "arms" without realizing it, talking past each other. So in what follows, pay close attention to *which* idea of god we are discussing.

Here's another source of confusion. God can be a specific name, as when we pray to the supreme being that Christians worship. But

God can also be a generic term. It might mean, for example, "that which is most sacred," which signifies different things to different people. It's easy to get mixed up about whether we are discussing something fairly well-defined, or asking, "Does anything exist that qualifies as a god?" I usually capitalize God in referring to a specific force or being, and use lower case for the generic idea of god.

Let's begin seeing why theism and atheism can be complementary rather than contradictory, by considering a simple idea that has far-reaching implications if we take it seriously:

> ❖ *The difference between belief*
> *and disbelief is often merely wordplay,*
> *a matter of semantics rather than substance.*

We depend so much on language that we sometimes focus on words rather than on the reality to which those words are pointing. If we look beyond words we will see that setting up a sharp dichotomy between theists and atheists is dangerous and superficial.

Think about the philosophy known as deism. Deism means belief in a god "who creates the world, ordains its laws, and then leaves it to its own devices."[88] In the U.S., George Washington, Benjamin Franklin, and Thomas Jefferson were deists. For most deists, God is an absentee creator who "does not respond to human prayer or need."[89] Arguably there isn't much practical, everyday difference between this sort of doctrine and atheism. Many deists have believed that we would meet God after death, but others have doubted or denied this claim. In fact a deist could maintain that God is just whatever it was that caused the Big Bang.

Let's say Joe and Moe agree that something caused the universe to appear and that we have little or no idea what it was.

Joe's sweatshirt says **Theist**. "God is whatever created the cosmos," he declares.

Moe waves the **Atheist** banner. "Something caused the cosmos, but why call it God?"

Different labels, different slogans, and yet so very much in common.

God and Nature

Some versions of deism, then, are close cousins of atheism. Atheism also overlaps with *naturalistic theism*. As the Rev. William Murry explains, naturalistic theists understand "God as belonging to the natural universe rather than as a supernatural deity."[90]

There are two ways to be a naturalistic theist. First, one might believe in a godlike power that is part of the universe but which science cannot currently detect. For example, one might define God as a collective consciousness that connects all minds. Science has not yet discovered such a consciousness, but maybe it will in the future. Second, some naturalistic theists revere something within nature as we currently understand it, something so precious they consider it sacred. For example, some say that God is the power of creativity in the universe, including the forces that generate new stars and the inventive capacities of the human mind. Others are in awe of the same creative forces, but without naming them God.[91] That makes them atheists or agnostics (unless they believe in some other sort of deity). The difference is merely verbal. We all have the right to speak in ways that makes sense to us.

One Garrison-Martineau participant pondered the connection between deity and creativity: "If there is a creative force, and there has to be one someplace, somehow, in some fashion, what is the nature of that creative force? Is it a conscious, personal God like Christians claim it is, or is it just a creative force that creates things?"[92]

In *Reason and Reverence,* William Murry lists several naturalistic god-concepts. God could be "the driving force of the natural world . . . the universal self in each person . . . the power for good in the world . . . 'the spirit' . . . the spirit of love" or just "mystery."[93] Richard Dawkins mentions the idea that God is "the ultimate" or "our better nature" or even the whole universe.[94] (He does not favor defining God in this way.) And Daniel Dennett has commented that "god" could be used as a name for human goodness. "It's super, and it's natural. It's just not supernatural."[95]

At times it's hard to know who is "really" a theist and who is an atheist. For example, let's say George is a Presbyterian. He sees God as the creative force that brought the universe into being. He believes this force must be good, because the universe is a basically good place. His God does not perform miracles or answer specific prayers, and George sees all the talk about having a relationship with a personal god as a poetic way of speaking. (Similarly, in a poetic sense I have a relationship with Mother Earth, even though Earth is not actually a person.) He knows this is an unorthodox viewpoint, but he loves the Bible and Presbyterian worship even though he interprets Christian doctrine metaphorically. George believes that when God created the world we were given all the gifts we would need. That is, the cosmos was created in a way that would eventually bring us the gift of life, the opportunity to love and be loved, a sense of wonder, and a wondrous world for our enjoyment. For George, that is more than enough to make God worthy of worship.

Compare George to Jennifer. Jennifer is an outspoken skeptic who loves atheist writers such as Sam Harris and says the idea of god is destructive. But Jennifer believes that life is an educational process. Good or bad things happen in order to teach us lessons that are intended for us personally. She doesn't have an explanation about how this occurs, but she says that this idea is validated by her own life-experience. "Things happen, to teach me what I need to know."

Which one is the believer and which one is the infidel? George's theology is deistic. God created the universe but now lets it run on its own without needing to intervene any further. By contrast, Jennifer does believe there are forces for good that intervene in our lives in highly specific ways. If Jennifer used the word "god" to speak of whatever is trying to teach us lessons, she would be a theist. Since she does not, she's an atheist. And yet in some ways she seems more theistic than George.

Here's another way that people may believe the same things but disagree about whether to use the word god: Many people conceive of God as a force rather than a person, while others believe in similar forces without using god-language to describe them. According to a Gallup poll, *nearly 30 percent* of those who live in North America think of deity as "some sort of spirit or life force" rather than as an invisible person.[96] One can call a life force God, or one can just call it a life force.

How do you react when you hear about deism, naturalistic theism, and non-personal ideas of God? Some readers will say, "Well of course. People think of God in lots of ways." Others will say, "Those who don't think of God as a person aren't thinking of deity at all. They shouldn't even use the word." Both responses are understandable because we have many opinions about how words should be used. In any event, when you hear that a certain percentage of the population believes in God, remember that this simple word unfolds into a very, very wide umbrella. Using one word to mean many different things has its advantages, but it can create the illusion of communication among people who are actually talking past each other. It can also conjure up the illusion of unanimity, when people are far from united.

Some in the clergy are hard to classify as either theists or atheists. For example, the Christian humanism of Anthony Freeman does not fit neatly into either category. I would not call him an atheist because he still finds the idea of deity meaningful. He values Christian stories and traditional religious language, including the word god.[97] He also continues to lead and participate in public worship. Nevertheless, Freeman is entirely naturalistic: "Today . . . a number of people are finding meaning in a non-supernatural version of Christianity . . . I can still benefit from using God religiously, without believing in him as an objective and active supernatural person."[98]

Freeman views God as "the sum of all my values and ideals in life."[99] He thinks of deity as a spiritually-resonant symbol rather than as an actual entity, and he is far from alone. Don Cupitt calls God "the mythical embodiment of all that one is concerned with in the spiritual life. He is the religious demand and ideal, the pearl of great price and the enshriner of values. He is needed – but as a myth."[100] And the Rev. Alexie Crane presents this paradox: "I am an atheist. I do not believe in God. Never did. But there is more. I also love God. I am an atheist who loves God . . . the word God serves as a symbol, a focus for the thoughts, feelings, and intuitions that go into our intimate, inward relation with the whole of reality, both known and unknown, seen and unseen."[101]

During the 1960's some radical theologians suggested that the word god had become so encrusted with outdated meanings that we should give it a rest for a few decades and then define it afresh. We can't take a word that does so much work for people and set it on the shelf, but we can expand religious discourse with new terminology. The Twelve-Step movement, beginning with Alcoholics Anonymous, has developed a new usage, a big-tent concept that covers diverse ideas without (usually) creating confusion.

Higher Powers

The founders of Alcoholics Anonymous felt that a religious awakening had saved them from alcoholism, but they also cared about alcoholics who were not traditionally religious. Alcoholics Anonymous' "big book" quotes an early A.A. participant who was reflecting on the way religion helps some people quit drinking:

"The word God still aroused a certain antipathy. . . . I could go for such conceptions as Creative Intelligence, Universal Mind or Spirit of Nature but I resisted the thought of a Czar of the Heavens, however loving His sway might be. . . . My friend suggested what then seemed a novel idea. He said, 'Why don't you choose your own conception of God?'"[102]

Instead of demanding that we accept some traditional theology, A.A. suggested that people rely on God *as we understand him*. That still sounds as if God is a person (and male), so eventually A.A. began to speak of "a higher power, however you choose to define it."

In the book, *Came to Believe,* A.A. members write about how they experience a higher power:

"The Upanishad, part of the Hindu scriptures, concludes: 'From Joy all things are born; by Joy all things are sustained; to Joy all things return.' The more thoroughly I can surrender to this proposition, the more thoroughly I enjoy my life. Ultimately, my God as I understand Him is joy and the expansion of the joy."

Another member spoke of A.A.'s Third Step, "Made a decision to turn our will and our lives over to the care of God *as we understood Him.*" This "can be a tough order . . . if one has some problems in the 'God' area, as I do. Rephrasing helped me quite a bit: 'God as I *don't* understand Him and 'over to the care of *Good.*'

"These two ideas let a heathen like me dismiss the religious question and begin to experience the spiritual benefits of A.A. . . . It was a great relief to me to learn that I simply didn't have to understand. After all, you don't have to know how a tree grows to make a fence out of wood."

Finally, an alcoholic from New York speaks of a life force rather than a personal deity. For him the ocean symbolizes this force, and his outlook could have been expressed as either theism or atheism:

"I come closest to [prayer] when I can contemplate an unbroken horizon from the deck of a ship. I am cut down to size; I feel serenely that I am a small part of something vast and unknowable.

"But isn't the ocean rather a cold symbol? Yes. Do I think that its eye is on the minnow, that it is concerned about any individual's fate? . . . Would I talk to it? No . . . *Is* there anything beyond the realm of human reason? Yes, I believe there is. Something."[103]

These statements show a marvelous flexibility and tolerance. Because the higher power concept is deliberately and explicitly diverse, members of Twelve-Step groups realize that one person's

HP may be quite different from another's. And in A.A. all higher powers share one essential feature – they provide extra support for abstaining from alcohol. Thus even theists and atheists share a common understanding when they speak in terms of a higher power.

Some people have criticized this idea, arguing that "higher" implies something separate from the self and is thus *disempowering,* leading us away from helpful inner resources. A friend of mine dealt with this issue by thinking of "a Deeper Power, accessing something within that's beyond my usual grasp that could help me to stay sober – something like a Life Instinct."

✎ *Your higher power.* If the higher power concept sounds useful, here's a way to apply it. Think about an area of your life where you seem to need some assistance, where despite your best efforts you have been unable to make much progress. Now, think of something that could help you, something or someone you can turn to when the chips are down. Then look for opportunities to find support, encouragement, insight, and inspiration from this source of strength.

Summing up: "God" is an octopus word, with meanings that stretch out in several directions. The question is not "Does God exist?" It's "Which god(s) exist, if any?"

Although some forms of theism are starkly incompatible with some forms of atheism, belief or disbelief is often a difference of semantics rather than substance.

Some think of God as a force rather than as a personal presence. Others believe in a force for good, but don't give it a religious label. Still others define deity as an aspect of nature – love, truth, creativity, humanity, mystery, the Earth, the laws of nature, or the entire universe. Others treasure the same things, without calling them God.

Chapter Seven
Mystery and Metaphor

We have seen that the "difference" between theism and atheism is sometimes just a difference in the way we use words. My next suggestion is much more radical. *I even see common ground between atheists and those who believe in God as a personal being, who thinks, feels, makes judgments, acts, and communicates.*

Such a deity is often called a *personal* god, and belief in a divine person can be called *personal theism.* It is a challenging task to show what atheism and this sort of theism have in common, and it will take me a while to make my case. But here is a key idea that breaks down the rigid barrier between personal theism and atheism:

❖ *When religion describes God as a person,*
this description is often meant symbolically or poetically
rather than literally.

I admit that some theists believe God is literally a super-person, very much like us except bigger and better. But many think of God's personhood as a metaphor, as spiritual poetry rather than factual prose. The great theologian Thomas Aquinas, for example, thought that we could only speak about God "indirectly, through analogy."[104] Analogical descriptions say that one thing is like something else: "The Lord is my shepherd," for instance, means that God's relationship to me is *like* a shepherd's relationship with sheep. Such analogies are helpful, but never perfect. God doesn't literally walk around carrying a shepherd's staff.

Some theologians who say that we cannot comprehend God seem to forget about that when they describe deity. They say, in effect, "God is entirely beyond human understanding! And now let me tell you all about this unfathomable mystery: God is eternal, all-knowing, all-powerful, the creator of the universe, perfect in every way, 100% loving and fair. Furthermore this being is a person, who thinks, feels, makes choices, hears and answers prayer, and performs miracles."

Do you see the problem? It seems very odd to present such a long list of specific claims, when it may be as hard for us to understand God as it would be for a poodle to master astrophysics.

Since our minds are decentralized and even fragmented, it is almost inevitable that some parts of a person's philosophy of life will contradict other aspects. Saying we can and cannot comprehend deity is a prime example. And remember the phenomenon of different route, different result. If we probe a person's beliefs by asking, "Do we understand God?" the answer may be "No! God is far beyond our grasp." But if we take a different route and ask, "What is God like?" all sorts of specific qualities may be stated. After affirming the divine mystery people slide right back into making definite claims about deity.

For a classic example of religious metaphor, think about Hinduism. Hindus are considered polytheists. There are over 300 million supernatural beings in their colorful pantheon. No doubt some Hindus accept polytheism literally, assuming that Vishnu, Kali, Ganesh, and all the others are real beings. But many Hindu scriptures construe these gods and goddesses as picturesque ways of representing the one creative spirit. This spirit is impersonal or transpersonal. Yet since we are persons, Hinduism speaks of deity in personal terms, which are easier to grasp.

Even when we sense that there are realities far beyond us, we want to think we grasp those realities. We may want so much to relate to the Great Mystery that we forget it is a mystery. So we decorate the divine darkness with elaborate doctrinal details. "People of faith admit in theory that God is utterly transcendent," comments Karen Armstrong, "but they seem sometimes to assume that *they* know exactly who 'he' is and what he thinks, loves, and expects."[105] Believers tend to emphasize God's personhood, while non-believers may try to cleanse the physical cosmos of any hint of mind or consciousness. Both theists and atheists experience the craving for certainty, the urge to tame unruly enigmas.

When we don't understand something well we may need to say, "In some ways, it's like *this*, but in other ways it's just the opposite." Such a two-sided (or multi-sided) view can be helpful, as long as we realize what we are doing and why. Thus people can legitimately say that God is incomprehensible and that God is a personal being – if they realize that each of these statements contains just part of the truth.

Thinking of God's personhood as a metaphor helps chip away the wall of separation between belief and unbelief. In the next sections I will expand on this idea, and then I will encourage atheists to consider ways that the universe itself may have personal characteristics. With any luck I'll have managed to make every reader "productively uncomfortable" by the end of this chapter.

God's Masquerade

If we say God is a person, what are we driving at? What *is* a person?[106] Personhood is an idea we use in talking about ourselves, based on the way we think humans operate. But as we have seen, this useful idea is oversimplified. For example, in some respects it makes sense to think of myself as a committee rather than as an "individual." The idea of personhood is a sort of mask that I put on in order to understand myself. This me-mask covers up a mind-boggling, ever-changing array of cellular and molecular activity, and perhaps a soul or spirit as well. And just as the idea of "me" is a simple face worn by a complex and internally diverse human organism, the idea of God may be a unifying mask which covers many great mysteries.

I realize that this discussion of personhood is rather abstract, so let's turn to some very obvious ways in which calling God a person is a poetic way of speaking. Persons like us have a certain sort of body, but a power or being that created the universe would not need toes or eyelashes. And what does it mean that God thinks? Human thoughts are shaped by the way our brains work. If God has no brain, how does this being process information? Ponder this intriguing passage from Isaiah 55:8-9:

> "For my thoughts are not your thoughts, neither are your ways my ways, says the Lord. For as the heavens are higher than the earth, so are my ways higher than your ways and my thoughts than your thoughts."

Using our limited powers of reasoning, how can we understand what it *means* that God thinks? Is "thinking" even the right word?

Similarly, in what sense does God care? Does God care in specific ways about specific people, or more like the Earth "loves" its creatures by being a generally supportive environment? Or in some other way that we cannot even imagine?

The Divine Feminine

Most of us grew up thinking in terms of a male supreme being, so thinking about God still tickles chains of neurons that were linked together long ago. These neural patterns conjure up the image of a majestic old graybeard, like Michelangelo's portrait of Yahweh in the Sistine Chapel. Importantly, when our brains add new god-patterns, these neural tracings cannot entirely erase the old ones. It is intriguing that in 2006, one-third of Americans still said God is male. Only one percent said God is female, and thirty-seven per-cent said "neither."[107] Since "neither" was an option, we may ask why so many chose "male" instead. Did they actually think that the Ultimate has male features? Big biceps? Facial hair? A deep voice? Etc?

Sometimes the answer is yes. According to a Harris Poll, about 10% of Americans say that God appears "like a human with a face, body, arms, legs, eyes."[108] But since a lot more than 10% say God is male, many people must think of God as a man but deny that God has a human body. Thus there is an inner contradiction in their concept of deity. Part of a person's mind can think of deity as a male human, while another part understands this as an analogy rather than a literal statement of fact.[109]

People are increasingly open to imagining God in female form, and this is gradually shifting the way we think of the supreme being/power/spirit. Parishioners have told me that picturing God with a woman's face brings important qualities into focus – love, compassion, gentleness, empathy, nurturance, affection, and commitment to children. Although these qualities are based on debatable stereotypes, it seems useful to expand our metaphors beyond stereotypical maleness. As the Rev. Roy Phillips commented, anybody who has only one image of the holy is committing idolatry.[110]

Some have drawn upon stories of the divine feminine from non-Abrahamic religions, such as the goddesses of European mythic traditions. Paganism may seem like a rather eccentric spiritual pathway, but most of the Neo-Pagans I have known see the feminine and polytheistic aspects of those traditions as thoroughly metaphorical. Just as no one today thinks that Zeus literally resides on Mount Olympus, few imagine that his wife, Hera, is a literally-existing entity.

So metaphor is crucial. One way to speak of deity without falling into literalism is to use the language of *as-if*. It is *as if* a higher power hears our prayers, thinks about them, and answers them. But it's hard to live in the fuzzy world of sorta-so. We would much rather think in definite, concrete terms. In practice, most theists will accept some specific description of what the Ultimate is like. Even so, it is good to remind ourselves that whatever lies hidden beneath the world that we see is a deep mystery, regardless of how we choose to label it.

It may be that standard descriptions of deity as perfect, eternal, and so on are elaborate ways of saying: *"God – Wow!"* Those who do not relate to god-language may feel a similar sense of amazement, a sort of Cosmic Wow. Thus both theism and atheism can point toward awesome mysteries far beyond our grasp. Regardless of whether we think the great unknown cares about us as individuals, regardless of whether it notices every sparrow's fall, it seems fitting to respond to it with wonder, and perhaps even reverence.

Theists, Atheists, Metaphor and Einstein

Theists are not the only ones who use word-pictures to speak of what is beyond our understanding. Many atheists and agnostics also use analogies and poetic images to describe the world. As Karen Armstrong remarks, astronomers realize that terms such as "big bang, dark matter, black holes, dark energy . . . are metaphors that cannot adequately translate their mathematical insights into words."[111] So even if we entirely replace religion with science, we are still encircled by metaphor.

Admittedly, atheists who are strongly oriented toward science do not typically think that the universe has personal characteristics. But this is only a subset of the entire atheist spectrum. Furthermore, Richard Dawkins notes that "A quasi-mystical response to nature and the universe is common among scientists and rationalists."[112] It is notoriously difficult to do justice to mystical experiences without using metaphor, and since we are persons we tend to use personal metaphors. Consider this famous statement by Albert Einstein:

"The most beautiful emotion we can experience is the mystical. It is the sower of all true art and science. . . . To know that what is impenetrable to us really exists, manifesting itself to us as the highest wisdom and the most radiant beauty, which our dull faculties can comprehend only in their most primitive forms – this knowledge, this feeling is at the centre of all true religiousness. In this sense, and in this sense only, I belong to the ranks of devoutly religious men."[113]

He also wrote, "That deeply emotional conviction of the presence of a superior reasoning power, which is revealed in the incomprehensible Universe, forms my idea of God."[114]

Einstein seems to have been a naturalistic theist. Although he called God a "reasoning power" and the "highest wisdom," he was using these words metaphorically. Unfortunately, the great man was caught in a tug-of-war between atheists and traditional theists. Both sides tried to draft him for their team, and he responded forcefully: "It was, of course, a lie what you read about my religious convictions, a lie which is being systematically repeated. I do not believe in a personal God and I have never denied this but expressed it clearly."[115] At the same time he disliked being pegged as an atheist: "In view of such harmony in the cosmos, which I, with my limited human mind, am able to recognize, there are yet people who say there is no God. But what really makes me angry is that they quote me for support of such views."[116]

When Einstein spoke of "wisdom" and "reasoning power," he did not intend these terms literally. But of course many theists who describe God in highly personalistic language are also speaking metaphorically. They may appreciate the familiar images of their own faith tradition – God as father, God as shepherd, God who holds me in the hollow of his hand – even though they suspect that these words can only hint at literal truth. If pressed to state their beliefs in literal terms, some of them might say something like this:

"God is ultimate reality – astonishingly mysterious, profoundly intelligent, beautiful, awe-inspiring, super-human, radically transcendent, and worthy of our deepest reverence. Beyond that, I can only speculate."

Such a statement would be quite similar to Einstein's views. So a lifestance that might at first sound like standard male-God theism may be closely akin to Einsteinian naturalism.

Having seen how Einstein's world-view resembles some forms of personal theism, let's turn in the opposite direction. What Einstein believed also overlaps with the outlook of many atheists, including Richard Dawkins. Both Einstein and Dawkins have reported a semi-mystical sense of wonder in contemplating the cosmos, and both have emphatically denied that the universe is personal in any literal sense. *So Einstein's beliefs overlapped with both atheists and personal theists.* Not with all atheists, of course, and not with all personal theists. But with many.

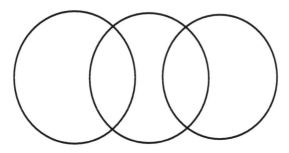

Einstein's Theism
Personal Theism   Atheism with a Sense of Awe

Are you seeing why it makes no sense to tidily divide the world into believers and non-believers?

Atheistic Metaphors

We will now consider four of the basic building blocks of personhood – thinking, creating, being conscious, and communicating. In each case, we will see that some atheists and agnostics speak of the universe and/or ultimate reality in semi-personal terms.

First of all, persons *think*, and the universe's order and lawful functioning is arguably a kind of intelligence. Remember Einstein's claim that a reasoning power is revealed in the universe. Many scientists have made similar comments. Taner Edis notes that "Physicists use 'God' as a metaphor more often than other scientists – especially in popular writing, but in the technical literature as well." The god-language of physicists seldom refers to a super-natural being. It is often "a metaphor for order at the heart of confusion."[117] Michael Dowd calls self-organization "an umbrella term that unites physicists, chemists, biologists, and computer scientists who are searching for what underlies the growth of order and complexity",[118] and self-organization is thought-like in the sense that it requires at least rudimentary information processing.

Quantum physicist David Bohm found "analogies between quantum processes and thought processes, thus carrying further the celebrated statement made by the astronomer James Jeans . . . 'Today . . . The universe begins to look more like a great thought than like a great machine . . . .'"[119] I'm not familiar with Bohm's and Jeans' theological views, but I know of dedicated atheists who agree that the universe has thought-like characteristics.

Natural selection through competition between species has been described as information *processing* without an information *processor*. In our own bodies the immune system is a sophisticated data-processor, even though it contains no brain. Plants lack central nervous systems, but they use information gleaned from their surroundings to guide their "actions." Thus sunflowers can follow the sun's daily journey. So much of our world is mindless, and yet mind-like.

In sum, one mark of personhood is the ability to think, and some atheists attribute thought processes to physical reality, either literally or metaphorically. As we learn more about the universe we may find that it processes information in large-scale, long-term ways that are amazing and unexpected.

Persons also *create*, and the universe is an overflowing cornucopia of creativity, spinning out vast galaxy-clusters like a cosmic Mozart pouring forth symphonies. Moreover, this seemingly mindless complex of matter and energy has produced humans, who consciously create.

Persons are *conscious,* and some atheists such as Sam Harris believe the entire universe may be aware, or semi-aware. (See Chapter Thirteen.) This idea is called panpsychism. Some kinds of panpsychism are related to the notion that there is "spiritual energy located in physical things such as mountains, trees or crystals." In a recent study, 26% of Americans endorsed this idea, no doubt including some atheists and agnostics.[120]

Another building block of personhood: Persons *communicate*, and so does the universe in either a poetic or literal sense. At times events and circumstances seem to speak quite forcefully, warning us or encouraging us. The consequences of bad decisions may seem like someone shouting in our ears. Earlier I mentioned an atheist who said certain things happen in order to teach her what she needs to know, and that was not just a hypothetical case. I have heard secular humanists make very similar statements.

Lots of people believe that in some subtle way, reality responds to our messages. They therefore try to influence future events by "sending out a positive intention," "holding a good thought," or visualizing favorable results. This strategy is akin to prayer, but it can also be interpreted non-theistically. We can act as if thoughts make a helpful difference even if we have no theory about how this transpires. Henry Stone, for example, has stated: "Although it's not part of the usual definition of atheism, I believe all our actions, words, and thoughts affect the structure of the universe. Our effect may be vanishingly small, but when many people act or think in unison, the effect is multiplied many times."[121] And Anthony Freeman, who does not believe that God is an existing being, thinks prayer may have powers we do not yet comprehend. He is "also open to the idea that in some natural (but as yet unexplained) way, the 'power of positive thought' can affect people and situations."[122]

Who knows what personal qualities we might discover in nature if we were better at understanding processes which are extremely large-scale or small-scale, dazzlingly rapid or glacially slow? I am reminded of the conclusion to "Big Sur Country," a poem by Ric Masten:

if we could speed time up
fast enough
we would see that the mountains
are dancing
and with us[123]

If you believe in God and you have an in-depth conversation with an atheist, don't be terribly surprised if he or she states that the universe manifests a creative and self-organizing intelligence, is conscious in ways that science does not yet understand, and may be responsive to human thoughts, emotions, and communications. The infidel may even declare that the cosmos is worthy of appreciation and awe. At that point you may want to blurt out, "So for you the cosmos is God!" No it is not. People use religious language in highly particular ways, and it is singularly unhelpful to tell others how to define deity.

Both theists and atheists, then, may think of reality in personal terms. Theists usually apply personal descriptions more literally, but there is no clear dividing line between literal and metaphorical language. *Poetry and factual description shade off into each other:*

God is a person who looks like us . . .
  God is a person but does not have a human body . . .
    Calling God a person is a human way of speaking
      about something far beyond our understanding . . .
        The Ground of All Being is trans-personal,
          but we can metaphorically think of it as a Thou . . .
            The universe is physical but it has personal qualities . . .
              The universe does not actually have such qualities, but
                we can speak poetically as if it does . . .
                  The universe, and whatever gave birth to it, should
                    never be thought of as personal.

People often shift and drift among these levels, sliding up or down this continuum as they switch from one sub-personality to another.

I want to emphasize the inevitable vagueness of our beliefs about all-that-is. Each person's belief-complex is a pastiche of factual information, informed and uninformed speculation, and poetic imagery. A theist, for example, might believe that a person-like God exists, realize that in at least some respects "person" is a metaphor, but be unable to say in what ways and to what extent God is actually a person. Similarly, some atheists see the universe as a mixture of personal and non-personal features.

How many theists have carefully thought about whether and in what respects God is "really" a person? And how many atheists and agnostics have carefully considered whether the cosmos (or whatever gave rise to the cosmos) has personal qualities? I suspect the answer to both questions is "very, very few." If they did contemplate these questions in depth, how often would believers and non-believers come to similar conclusions? I don't know, nor does anyone else, and that is the point. We simply have no idea how much similarity is hidden by divisive theological labels. Without in-depth dialogue about religion, we can never hope to understand each other.

We Need Both Perspectives

How shall we respond to the staggering strangeness of the universe? We could say, "Life's mystery is so dark that I would rather look where there is at least a little light. I'll focus on this planet and the creatures that live on it, and I will let worlds beyond this world take care of themselves." Or we could say, "The darkness of the great unknown is so fascinating, so inviting, that I must respond with awe, wonder, and worship. If I can grasp even one percent more of what lies within the divine darkness, that will justify many years of prayer and contemplation." (And of course, many people combine these approaches.)

Theism and atheism are two ways of articulating our responses to ultimate mystery. And here is a key idea that is obviously true but difficult to fully accept:

> ❖ *There is no objective place*
> *where we can stand and say,*
> *"Now I can see who is right about deity."*

Of course, many people believe they have attained objective truth about God. Some say it is quite clear that God is real. Others find it equally clear that atheism is correct. But there is no "tie-breaker," no super-objective vantage point that settles this dispute. No one can rise above the fray and consider this issue from a "god's-eye" perspective. We want to avoid this unsettling but undeniable conclusion. Honestly admitting that no one knows the truth about god is likely to make us squirm (unless we happen to be agnostics).

Wouldn't it be wonderful to have certainty about such an important question, so that all people who are good, smart, and well-informed would agree? But that is not where we find ourselves. We cannot dismiss the testimony of either believers or unbelievers.

> ❖ **When we put together the totality of human experience,**
> **we need both theism and atheism to reflect**
> **what we have seen on our journey thus far.**

> ❖ **Yes, there are differences between believing or not**
> **believing in a god that has personal qualities.**
> ***But belief and disbelief can meet on***
> ***the common ground of Mystery.***

People of many different world-views can link hands, by focusing on the great unknown.

Daniel Dennett and conservative commentator Dinesh D'Souza once engaged in a lively videotaped interchange about God's existence. At one point D'Souza emphasized that God's existence cannot be conclusively proven. In that sense, he said, both he and Dennett are agnostics. "I don't know, and still I believe. Dan doesn't know, and therefore, he doesn't believe. What unites us is both of us don't know. We're actually both ignorant. . . . We are both reasoning in the dark."[124]

I agree with D'Souza. We are all just staring off into the infinite unknown. Many think that this unfathomable abyss has personal or semi-personal qualities. Others maintain that we should think impersonally, in terms of an It rather than a Thou. So we make our choice – yes, there is a person-like god hidden in the darkness, or no, there is not. A contemporary hymn called "Bring Many Names" praises the "joyful darkness far beyond our seeing."[125] Both theists and atheists are speculating about the fertile darkness, which has somehow given us the astonishing gifts of life, love, and con-sciousness. When we realize how perplexing life is, we may agree that all opinions about ultimate reality are spiritual wagers, "leaps of faith" into belief or "leaps of doubt" into unbelief.

In short, *mystery-affirming theists and mystery-affirming atheists are brothers and sisters in disguise.*

At this point we have considered several ways to bridge the gap between theism and atheism. We can challenge the human tendency to worship our own opinions. We can learn to catch ourselves shutting our minds to new ideas that disturb our preconceptions. We can admit that both belief and disbelief are endorsed by thoughtful and well-intentioned individuals, and there is no way to know for certain who is right. And we can see that theism and atheism overlap in subtle and unexpected ways.

When we say God thinks and feels, we are trying to make familiar clothing fit an enigma whose size and shape we cannot discern. If we dress this mystery in god-language we are theists. If we do not use such language we are atheists, vilified as self-centered, materialistic, or even criminal. *To divide up the world in this way is simplistic, misleading, and destructive.* Do not assume that you understand another person's philosophy of life just because you know what label the person likes to wear. Go beyond the slogan on the sweatshirt. Explore the actual content of people's beliefs and the experiences that have led to these commitments.

The hidden kinship between belief and disbelief is exemplified by the marriage of two people I mentioned earlier, Michael Dowd and Connie Barlow. Connie and Michael have coined the term "cre-atheism," a single word with dual pronunciations. Dowd is a theist, so he pronounces it cree-uh-*THEISM*. Connie is an atheist, so she pronounces it cree-*ATHEISM*.[126] By emphasizing different parts of this term, they change its content while retaining an underlying commonality. This is a fine metaphor for the challenge of expressing individual beliefs while honoring our connections with others.

Summing up: There can be considerable common ground between atheists and personal theists. Religions which call God a person also say that God transcends our understanding, and some non-believers speak of ultimate reality in semi-personal terms.

There is no objective place where we can stand and say, "Now I see who is right about deity." We need both theism and atheism to reflect what we have found so far in our human quest for truth.

Although there are differences between believing or not believing in a god who has personal qualities, belief and disbelief can meet on the common ground of mystery. Mystery-affirming theists and mystery-affirming atheists are brothers and sisters in disguise.

I'll close this chapter with a unifying comment by the Rev. Nick Cardell:[127]

> Whether I am an accident of nature
> or the design of a god,
> it is I who must give dignity to my life
> if I am to be worthy of the design
> or build upon the accident.

THE ISSUES

Chapters Eight through Eleven:

Is God Real?
Do We Need God?
God and Morality
God and Mortality

Chapter Eight
Is God Real?

Having seen that some theisms have a lot in common with some atheisms, we will now grapple with reasons for believing or disbelieving in God. I hope that the following chapters will help theists, atheists, and agnostics understand each other better. People of all faiths and philosophies have important reasons for thinking as they do, reasons that others should not lightly dismiss.

At this point we will set aside the sort of naturalistic theism that sees God as part of nature. Instead we will consider whether God exists as a being, spirit, or force that is beyond the current grasp of science. I will say little about traditional proofs of the existence of God.[128] Few people have sufficient patience to analyze these proofs in detail, and few philosophers or theologians see them as compelling. But even without absolute proof, one can offer arguments and evidence about issues such as the following:

Is God real or imaginary?

Did God create the universe?

Is God person-like? In what ways and to what extent?

Does God communicate with us? Punish and reward us? Keep us alive after we die?

Does God help people? How? By intervening in specific ways or by exercising a more general influence? Does God answer prayer?

Is God perfect, all-powerful, all-knowing, good in every way, and everlasting (or beyond time)?

Dealing with these questions could be tediously academic, and I don't want *Bridging the God Gap* to read like a textbook. For the sake of variety I will shift to a conversational format half a dozen times, conveying religious ideas through three fictional characters. These characters are composite voices, based upon conversations from my work as a minister and psychotherapist. Theodore is a theist; Althea is an atheist. The third person, Agnes, has a T-shirt which reads: *"MILITANT AGNOSTIC – I don't know and you don't either."* Actually Agnes would like to be a believer, and most of the time her skepticism is rather gently expressed.

I have imagined this trio as good friends who can bluntly disagree without alienating each other. All three can cite facts and quotations that support their positions. I do not endorse everything they say, and some of their arguments are flawed. At times they make disrespectful comments, but they are generally gracious enough to admit being rude and apologize.

To get the most out of these dialogues pay particular attention to what the "other side" says. Notice what happens when you encounter a good idea that disturbs your preconceptions. What emotions do you feel? What impulses do you experience? At such uncomfortable moments it's only human to look for an exit: "I'd better go catch up on my emails."[129]

"In the Beginning . . ."

Ancient peoples tended to assume that there were only two possible explanations for the existence of heaven and Earth. Either "everything just happened" or "God(s) did it," and the latter seemed far more likely. Although they realized there was a lot they didn't know, it did not occur to them that their limited understanding also limited their awareness of alternatives.

Physics and biology have already given us another candidate: The universe radiated outward from the Big Bang and life-forms evolved through natural selection. Some of us agree with these theories and some do not, but at least they offer a conceivable alternative. So now we have at least four options rather than two: "it just happened," "a Creator made it," "Big Bang plus evolution," or a combination in which God caused the Big Bang and included evolution in the divine plan. Importantly, future scientists and philosophers may develop other credible theories about how the cosmos could be "a watch without a watchmaker." And of course, even if we had a million legitimate options, the right answer might still be, "God did it."

Let's see what our three friends have to say about this topic. Theodore leads off.

Theodore: Even if I try to convince myself that the universe could have appeared out of nowhere, it just doesn't seem plausible. Everywhere I look I find intricate order and regularity. Unbelievably complicated systems have to work with finicky precision for me to stay alive a single second. To me all of this just screams *"intelligent design!"* Don't either of you ever feel that way?

Althea: Of course it's hard to imagine how everything could function without an invisible guiding hand. But it's hard for me to imagine a great many things that have been well-established. I am only a moderately intelligent mammal living on a little planet near a smallish sun. Why should I be able to comprehend how the whole universe works?

Agnes: We're just a bunch of curious little critters trying to grasp infinite subtlety and complexity. Even so, I prick up my ears when I hear that physicists have found evidence of creative intelligence. Remember that YouTube video of the debate between Daniel Dennett and Dinesh D'Souza? D'Souza claimed that if certain cosmic laws had been infinitesimally different, "we would have no universe. We would have no life."[130] He concludes that a creative intelligence wanted us to be here, and some scientists agree with him.[131] This is one reason I'm an agnostic instead of an atheist. I'm still hoping God is real.

Althea: Right, but Dennett pointed out that there may be lots of other universes which operate according to laws that prevent life from occurring.[132] Some cosmologists even say there could be an *infinite* number of universes. Life might be impossible in almost all of these systems, but some of them might be suitable homes for living creatures. If these creatures didn't know about all the other universes, it would seem as if "the" universe was specifically designed for their benefit. "Wow, how come everything is arranged so precisely? I guess there must be a God!"

Theodore: I get laughed at as a religious person for believing in fairy-tale mythologies. But when scientists dream up wild stories about a universe-seeding mechanism that spits out an infinite number of cosmic systems, all the secular humanists solemnly nod and agree. There is only one reason these bizarre multiple-universe scenarios get any press. People see that if this is actually the only universe, it looks like it was fine-tuned to an astonishing degree *in order to make our existence possible.* Someone wanted us to be here.

Agnes: And perhaps wanted creatures on many other planets.

Theodore: Exactly. Life! That is genuine evidence of intelligent design, folks! When I try to imagine that it all just happened at random, it just doesn't make sense. This is not a faith-based argument. The idea of a godless cosmos *offends my intelligence.* I had a logic teacher in college who often spotted a fallacious argument just by noticing that it sounded fishy. He relied more on hunches than on tight little syllogisms. His mind was equipped with a built-in nonsense-detector that sounded an alarm, and an alarm goes off in my mind when people claim that all this wonderment happened for no reason at all.

Althea: Theodore, my nonsense-detector is ringing so loud it hurts my ears. You are forgetting what is completely obvious. SOMETHING basic and wondrous did have to happen for no reason we can ever know, whether it was the universe itself or a hidden reality which gave birth to the universe.

Agnes: People who say God made the universe don't ask where God came from, because they don't know how to even begin thinking about something so far beyond their own experience. They just shrug their shoulders and change the subject. As Steven Wright says, "A conclusion is the place where you got tired of thinking."

Theodore: Nevertheless there are brilliant scientists and philosophers who say that it looks like the whole shebang was set up as a home for creatures like us.

Agnes: This is all speculation on top of speculation. Sure, some scientists say the universe seems to have been designed to enable life to exist, but other scientists disagree. It's easy to go on TV and proclaim that "researchers believe Blah Blah Blah," but there is no clear consensus about this issue.[133] I have a sneaking suspicion that in ten years, or ten thousand years, a bunch of sheepish physicists will publish an apologetic news release: "Sorry, everyone. We now realize that there are an unbelievably large number of ways that a universe could support intelligent life. For one thing, 'intelligent life' doesn't need to be anything at all like us. Please disregard our previous statements about this matter."

Althea: Besides, if a super-duper mind created the universe, why would it resemble our traditional concepts of God? It would have to be an incredible information-processing system with the power to shape matter, but look at all the ways that a matter-shaping mind might *not* be godlike. It might not be conscious. It might have no emotions, and no sense of right and wrong. It might be unaware of (or uninterested in) *Homo sapiens*. It might not be eternal, and in fact it might not even exist anymore. "It" might be several different entities, working together. Its attention might even be focused on some other universe, and our cosmos might be an accidental by-product of what it's doing "over there."[134]

Theodore: Regardless, when I try to think about the universe reasonably, I reject the idea of existence without an intelligent cause. To me *that* is nonsense, pure and simple. If I am going to use my own reason, I can't ignore what my reason is telling me.

Agnes: Theodore, I agree with you that there is evidence of intelligent design. I do find that intriguing, and I'd like to believe that it proves there is a god. But I agree with Althea that if we claim that the world had a cause, and call that cause God, we are only substituting one puzzle for another. Why not just assume that the world has no cause? Some physicists, such as Stephen Hawking, say that a causeless cosmos makes excellent sense.[135] It seems backwards to drag in a mysterious extra entity in order to solve a mystery. Something must exist for no reason, either God or the cosmos.

🙢 🙢 🙢 🙢 🙢 🙢 🙢 🙢 🙢 🙢 🙢 🙢 🙢 🙢

Reviewing this discussion, which statements felt right to you? Which ones seemed far-fetched? What comments sounded reasonable even though they contradicted what you tend to believe? The controversy about how the cosmos began is a classic example of the way people can look at similar data and reach diametrically opposite conclusions.

Science Versus Supernaturalism

Some people become atheists because they see contradictions between religion and the scientific world-view. This is no problem for those who revere some marvelous aspect of nature and call it God, but it does pose challenges for personal theism. We now rejoin the conversation:

Agnes: It's hard for me to imagine that our physical world is constantly interacting with invisible gods, angels, and demons. If that were so, scientists would notice it. "What's going on?" they would ask. "Why don't our experiments come out right? Something's happening that we haven't plugged into our calculations." But every time they come across some weird result, they find a purely physical explanation for it. Although there will still be unsolved problems at any given time, the trend toward physical solutions is clear.

Theodore: So are you saying that if science can't locate God, God doesn't exist? Come on, Agnes, we can't expect to find God as if he were a physical object. There are simple ways to tell whether a rhinoceros is living in my backyard, but there isn't any simple deity-detecting system. We only know God when he reveals himself to us.

Althea: Obviously I agree with Agnes, here, and it's not just that we can't detect deity easily. Quarks aren't easily detected either. But unlike quarks, God is not *reliably* discoverable. Some people think they have encountered a super-being and some do not.

Theodore: And some people hear sounds that others cannot.

Althea: And some see giant polka-dotted porcupines. Look, no offense, but I think theists have very vivid imaginations. They want to believe that a loving spirit watches over them, so they convince themselves it's true.

Theodore: OK, Althea, "no offense," but maybe your ability to imagine anything beyond your physical senses is unusually weak. When I say I am in touch with something beyond the material world I am in good company with billions of other people. Remember that atheists are a small minority.

Althea: We do not establish metaphysics by majority vote!

Theodore: Of course not, but you can't just write off the beliefs of enormous numbers of people, for centuries, all over the world.

Agnes: Here in the U.S. very few people say they do not believe in a personal God. But in Canada around 20 or 30% are atheists or agnostics. In the U.K. it's about 30-45%, and 65% in Japan.[136]

Althea: On another subject, Theodore, when you pray, how do you know you're getting a response? You can touch a daisy to check whether it's real or a plastic fake, but praying doesn't have reliable results. The cliché is that God always answers prayer and sometimes the answer is "no," but that's "heads I win tails you lose." If you get what you prayed for, the prayer was answered. If not, you weren't praying for the right thing!

Agnes: Then you're left wondering, "Wait a second, where is this marvelous divine intervention when I need help NOW?" I think of Woody Allen's famous complaint: "Not only is there no god, but try getting a plumber on weekends."

Theodore: Prayer is not like a vending machine for instant miracles. But I can feel God here with us now, just as clearly as knowing there's a ceiling on this room. It's not exactly like seeing, of course, but it's a definite sensing, a clear and tangible kind of contact. And here is something important: When I use the spiritual practices of my church, this sense of presence deepens. It's like learning to use a telescope better and better.

Althea: But when I look in your "telescope," I don't see a thing.

Theodore: Althea, I think you bought a broken scope! Or maybe you just glance in it, get nervous, and turn away. And speaking of things that can't be reliably verified, how could we possibly know that atheists are trying as hard as theists to connect with God? When's the last time you spent even one hour in prayer?

Agnes: On the other hand, even though science has never found God, it may happen eventually. We can detect things from their effects even though we can't observe them directly. Scientists locate a black hole by noticing its effects on nearby objects. If invisible spirits make a real difference in our lives, we might discover that something unseen is intervening in human affairs.

Science has already investigated seances, ghost sightings, and visions of deceased loved ones.

Althea: Right, and it all turns out to be bunk.

Agnes: Not always. But my point is that there's nothing bizarre about proving God's existence this way. Suppose hundreds of people had dreams in which dead relatives told them they were delivering messages from God. And suppose these messages provided information that no one alive possesses, like the way to make a medicine that cures cancer. Wouldn't that count as evidence of a higher intelligence?

Althea: If that happened I'd have to rethink my atheism, but it's not going to happen.

Theodore: Is this the same Althea who is always preaching at me that I should keep an open mind?

Althea: You're missing my point. I said I *would* rethink my atheism if Agnes' fantasy came true, and I also predicted I won't have to do that. I'd rethink my opinion of my husband if he turned out to be a bigamist, a drug lord, or an Iranian spy, but those odd possibilities don't worry me.

Agnes: Scientists have studied whether prayer helps sick people recover, but the results are mixed.[137] One Columbia University experiment seemed to prove that women with fertility problems became pregnant twice as often if they were prayed for, but the study turned out to be fraudulent.[138] Unfortunately people sometimes lie, perhaps to promote a belief-system, to advance themselves professionally, or just to feed their own egos. Prayer may work, but you can't prove that with just a few investigations. We have to see a consistent pattern.

Althea: We can always do more studies, but I am an atheist partly because so many reasons for belief in God have been superceded by science. People used to explain everything they didn't understand by saying God did it, but this gives us a "god of the gaps." The gaps keep getting smaller and the gap-god keeps shrinking.

Theodore: For once I agree with you, Althea. I do not go to church to get easy answers to unsolved problems. In fact I am offended by those who throw unanswered questions into God's great lap, treating the Lord like a bottomless celestial wastebasket. Rather than indulging in this sort of speculation I base my faith on direct personal experience. I know my Creator is with me, and I know this right here and now as we sit around chatting about whether he exists.

❧ ❧ ❧ ❧ ❧ ❧ ❧ ❧ ❧ ❧ ❧ ❧ ❧ ❧

Let's pick up on Theodore's last statement, turning to a crucial argument for God's existence that some find compelling and others dismiss.

Feeling God's Presence

Countless individuals testify that they have clearly and vividly experienced the presence of God. How do we evaluate such experiences? Some encounters are subtle, as when John Wesley, the founder of Methodism, found that his heart was "strangely warmed."[139] Others are dramatic, as when Paul was reportedly struck blind while hearing the voice of Jesus.[140]

Someone who has frequent impressions of God's presence could argue that this data is just as reliable as seeing rocks, trees, and animals. Furthermore, this sense of presence is extremely common. Could so many people be mistaken?

"This argument from personal experience is the one that is most convincing to those who claim to have had one," asserts Richard Dawkins, "But it is the least convincing to anyone else, and anyone knowledgeable about psychology." He compares such beliefs with psychotic delusions. When individuals claim to be, say, Napoleon, we dismiss their delusions, "mostly because not many people share them. Religious experiences are different only in that the people who claim them are numerous."[141]

Having been a psychotherapist, I am puzzled at the idea that no one knowledgeable about psychology would see evidentiary value in religious experiences. How can that be, when so many mental health professionals belong to churches, temples, and mosques? Certainly some of these believers would consider religious experiences to be a source of spiritual insight. I myself do not typically have exotic religious visions, but when so many people are convinced that they are in contact with invisible spirits I cannot disregard their testimony.[142]

Mystical experiences are particularly important. Psychologist William James describes these as brief episodes in which one feels grasped by a powerful force or being. One may seem to be in direct contact with profound truths – intuitively perceiving the unity of all things, for example. Such experiences are typically intense, emotionally positive, and extremely meaningful. Mystics often say that words cannot describe these events, and that all verbal descriptions should be understood as metaphorical.

Eric Reitan believes that such experiences offer evidence of a transcendent reality which has both the power and the desire to fulfill our deepest hopes. He says the typical features of mystical episodes are exactly what we would expect if mystics were in contact with a loving and powerful deity.[143]

Daniel Dennett, an atheist, has tried to empathetically articulate the positive glow of sensing God's presence. He says that from a theist's point of view, God's presence is "a joy warmer than the joy of motherhood, . . . more ecstatic than the joys of playing or singing great music. . . . We *know*, then, that God is the greatest thing that could ever enter our lives. It isn't like accepting a conclusion; it's like falling in love."[144] Compare this comment by the Rev. Marni Harmony: "How do you prove God? How do you prove love? . . . One feels God . . . and then one knows."[145]

If atheists want to explain religious experience without dismissing it out of hand, they could emphasize the idea that *an experience is not a belief.* Many theological doctrines are based upon extraordinary phenomena such as visions, dreams, trances, revelations, and religious conversions. But such phenomena are usually ambiguous, as open to interpretation as an abstract painting or a Rorschach ink blot.[146] Several different individuals could have exactly the same inner experience, but explain it in contradictory ways.

To conclude after a mystical vision that "What I experienced was God" involves thoughts, words, and concepts. Without an interpretation there would be no way to conceptualize and articulate such an occurrence. The best one could do would be to grunt, sing, laugh, or cry out.

Let's say that seven people who are dealing with personal life crises suddenly feel a profound and unexpected serenity. One of the seven interprets the experience as the presence of God. Another believes it was a spirit guide. Others say it was a message from the collective unconscious, or from the higher self, or the voice of reason, or it was caused by taking vitamins. Or it was simply a change in mood that requires no explanation.

Since spiritual experiences are hard to put into words, it is not surprising that people interpret them in familiar terms. As Anthony Freeman notes, a Roman Catholic may report seeing the Virgin Mary, but few Protestants report Mary-visions.[147] A Hindu mystic is unlikely to say, "I saw Jesus," and it would be noteworthy if a Christian saw Mother Kali. Even to say that one has experienced

God is an interpretation, and not all mystics draw this conclusion. Probably some theistic mystics and some atheistic mystics have had very similar experiences but choose to describe them differently.

If you are confident that you have experienced God, it will be difficult for atheists to dissuade you. If you are an atheist, it will be difficult for theists to convince you that their private states of consciousness disclose the deep nature of reality. The crucial point is that each of these opinions can seem compellingly true from a certain perspective.

By comparison, think about premonitions. Many people say they have anticipated future events which came to pass. If this sort of thing happened to you over and over, wouldn't you believe that premonitions are real? Wouldn't it be hard for someone to talk you out of it? But those who do not experience premonitions might dispute the claim that others can peer into the future. What's more, our egos become involved. Those who lack premonitions don't want to think they are defective. Those who do believe in premonitions don't want to think they have been kidding themselves. Similarly, theists don't want to think they are misinterpreting their own experiences, and atheists don't want to be told that they are inferior deity-detectors.

Once again, it's a standoff.

❖ **Believing that people do or do not feel God's presence is a classic case of dueling intuitions.**

✎ Think back to some of your own "peak experiences" – special states of mind that gave you a fresh outlook on life, regardless of whether you interpreted them religiously. These may or may not have involved a sense of divine presence.

What seemed to call forth these extraordinary states of mind? What aspects of these episodes would you like to keep fresh and alive? How could you encourage similar breakthroughs in the future? If you are traditionally religious, can you imagine construing these experiences in non-religious terms? If you are an atheist or agnostic, can you imagine someone else being in a similar frame of mind and considering it religiously significant?

Could God Be Real Without Existing?

As I mentioned earlier, people talk about "existence" in several ways. Karen Armstrong, for example, emphasizes that God does not exist. "Jewish, Christian, and Muslim theologians have insisted for centuries that God does not exist and that there is 'nothing' out there . . . ."[148]

Many traditional religious leaders are startled by this claim. Albert Mohler, president of Southern Baptist Theological Seminary, brands Armstrong as an atheist.[149] And Richard Dawkins speaks of theologians who "say something like this: 'Good heavens, of course we are not so naive or simplistic as to care whether God exists. . . . It doesn't matter whether God exists in a scientific sense. What matters is whether he exists for you or for me.'"

"Well, if that's what floats your canoe, you'll be paddling it up a very lonely creek," Dawkins admonishes. Most believers say God truly exists, "just as surely as the Rock of Gibraltar exists."[150]

James Wood concurs. "Theologians and priests are always changing the game in this way. They accuse atheists of wanting to murder an overliteral God, while they themselves keep alive a rarefied God whom no one, other than them, actually believes in."[151]

If God is real but does not exist, how could we even begin to describe deity? Armstrong answers this question by maintaining that the Ultimate is indescribable. We "don't understand what we mean when we say that he is 'good,' 'wise,' or 'intelligent.'"[152] At times she seems to suggest that the best description of deity would consist of an extended silence.[153]

I agree that if there is a God, we know far less about this force or spirit than we might like to imagine. Even so, the notion that we can say nothing about deity seems like a kissing cousin of atheism. Suppose I tell you I believe in a *whatsis,* and that the whatsis is quite important to me. "What's a whatsis?" you ask, and I say I do not know. You have a hunch I am talking about something like an invisible spirit. No, I say, calling it a spirit doesn't fit. Is it a being, then? That doesn't fit either, I reply. Well, what does it *do?* Again, I have no idea.

By this point you would suspect that even though the whatsis matters a great deal to me, it does not seem to have any sort of actuality (except in my head). The atheist in Charles Taliaferro's *Dialogues about God,* puts it bluntly: "If logic . . . or ideas can make no sense of God, then the concept of God is nonsense . . . I see this conclusion as essentially my own: the assertion there is no God."[154]

I would hazard a guess that Karen Armstrong would affirm some things about the Ultimate, including qualities such as creativity, transcendence, and some sort of goodness. And I certainly applaud her effort to correct overly-literal theologies. Her many books have conclusively proven that spiritual teachers throughout history have considered God beyond human comprehension. That is such a refreshing contrast to those who think they know everything about deity except (perhaps) the Lord's favorite pizza toppings.

If we say God is indescribable, here are three things that this might mean.

1. Something is indescribable if we can say virtually nothing about it. For instance, some think the Big Bang must have had a cause, but they haven't a clue what that was. All they know is that it triggered what little Calvin (in the Calvin and Hobbes comic strip) called The Horrendous Space Kablooie.[155]

2. On the other hand, "indescribable" may just mean we lack a good description. In some cases we can make many accurate statements about something, but even in combination these statements are pitifully incomplete. Suppose someone grabs an elephant's leg in the dark and thinks it's a tree. Even if the beast held still long enough for this leg-seizer to make 50 accurate statements about this massive limb, those statements would not add up to a good description of the elephant.[156]

3. Finally, "indescribable" may be mere hyperbole, dramatic exaggeration for effect. After one's first sexual encounter, one may exclaim, "Words fail me! All I can say is 'Wow!'" – after which one scrawls pages of intimate descriptive detail in a diary.

So God could be utterly indescribable, partially describable, or "indescribable" as poetic exaggeration. In my opinion, many who say it's impossible to describe deity would accept the second alternative: We know a lot about the Ultimate, but there is a great deal more that we do not know.

If you'd like to explore your own ideas about God's existence, you might try the following exercise.

✎ *Pro and Con: Is There a God?* By using the radial outline format or by making a list, write down what you see as the strongest arguments for and against the existence of God. Start by deciding which sort of deity you'll be considering, e.g., the God of the Christian Bible. List arguments for God's actuality on one side and arguments against on the other. I've included an outline that is drawn from a pastoral counseling session.

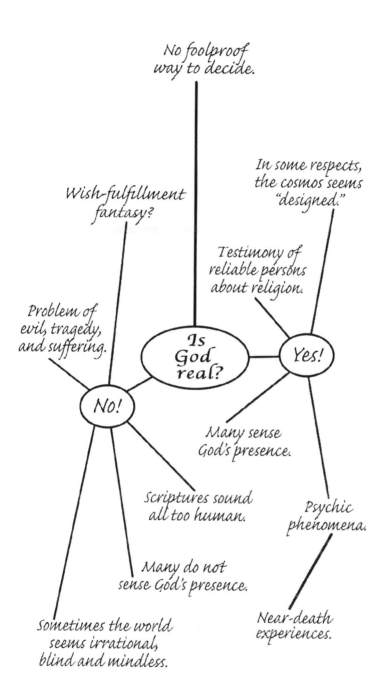

No foolproof
way to decide.

In some respects,
the cosmos seems
"designed."

Wish-fulfillment
fantasy?

Testimony of
reliable persons
about religion.

Problem of
evil, tragedy,
and suffering.

**Is
God
real?**

Yes!

No!

Many sense
God's presence.

Scriptures sound
all too human.

Psychic
phenomena.

Many do not
sense God's presence.

Sometimes the world
seems irrational,
blind and mindless.

Near-death
experiences.

Summing up: Although physics and biology offer explanations for the unfolding of the cosmos and the origin of species, many people feel there must be a creative intelligence behind it all.

Some people become atheists because religion doesn't fit their understanding of science. Others incorporate the scientific world-view into theism.

Feeling God's presence is one of the most common and compelling bases of belief, but religious experience can be given many interpretations. We find ourselves with dueling intuitions, and no clear winner either way.

Chapter Nine
Do We Need God?

The conflict between theism and atheism is not just about whether God exists. People also argue about whether belief in God helps us or hurts us, and in this chapter we will begin considering this question. Chapters Ten and Eleven continue the discussion, focusing on whether we need God to live moral lives and to ease the fear of death. I will try to show why intelligent, well-informed men and women disagree about such matters.

Is Disbelief Depressing?

Many people find theism far more appealing than the alternative. They may shudder at the bleak picture painted by Richard Dawkins in *River Out of Eden*: "The universe we observe has precisely the properties we should expect if there is, at bottom, no design, no purpose, no evil and no good, nothing but blind, pitiless indifference."[157]

If taken out of context, however, this quotation hints at personalistic connotations which Dawkins does not intend. When we say someone or something is "pitiless," this conveys a sense of coldness and cruelty, as in describing a terrorist or a serial killer. If a newscaster says, "the hurricane lashed Miami with pitiless force," these words evoke subtly malevolent images, as if hostile eyes were peering out of the windstorm. Even to call the universe "indifferent" may suggest that a gigantic being is staring down at us, contemptuous of our antlike insignificance. We read personal qualities into all sorts of natural phenomena.

River Out of Eden actually contends that nature is "neither cruel nor kind." Furthermore Dawkins wrote this book "to accord due recognition to the inspirational quality of our modern understanding of Darwinian life."[158] Like many atheists he thinks of the universe as utterly impartial, but responds to it with amazement and delight.

The idea that atheism is a depressing lifestance is a key to Eric Reitan's case for Christian faith. Rather than claiming to prove God's existence, Reitan tries to present enough evidence to show that belief is a valid option. Such evidence gives us grounds for hoping "the universe is fundamentally on the side of goodness." God's existence would fulfill this hope. Reitan deplores the prospect of a world "*without* life, *without* personality, *without* a capacity to care . . . ." But if God exists, our world is "situated in a grander context . . . ."[159]

Let's assume that Theodore, Althea, and Agnes are familiar with Dawkins and Reitan, and see what they have to say. Remember, these dialogues are not meant to model ideal logic or optimal communication techniques. They are intended to show that theists, atheists, and agnostics all have important reasons for believing as they do.

Theodore: Belief in God makes sense to me, and without God the world would be a useless swirl of randomly generated fluff, devoid of meaning and value.

Agnes: But if theism didn't make sense to you, would you still believe, just to avoid facing an unpleasant reality?

Theodore: If I thought there was no God I'd be an atheist, but I wouldn't like it.

Althea: I admit that when I lost faith in God I felt a sort of "cosmic loneliness." The sky seemed strangely vacant. But any big change takes getting used to, and now I see my atheism as positive.

Agnes: How so?

Althea: I have received a great deal in return for losing deity. As the Rev. David Bumbaugh points out, humanism has given "us an immensely richer, longer, more complex history" which "provides a story rooted not in the history of a single tribe or a particular people, but a history rooted in the sum of our knowledge of the universe itself."[160] This expands my vision of what life is all about.

Theodore: Sure, but religion can accept every bit of this new knowledge without abandoning faith. We needn't set up a battle between science and religion.

Althea: In any case, my atheism does not strip away love, caring, or meaning. People talk as if life's meaning has to be written in the stars or handed down by Jehovah on stone tablets. But we can experience meaning without being big like the universe or old and powerful like some mythical god. Size, age, and power have nothing to do with it. We are small and our lives are brief, and yet each of us can experience love, beauty, wonder, and everything else that makes life worthwhile.

Theodore: But what about people who are facing tragedy? A friend of mine recently said, "My husband just went to Afghanistan for another combat tour. I was brought up to trust in Jesus and the resurrection. Can you see why I need to keep believing these things?" Why should this woman focus on any doubts she may have about Christianity? And what about those who live in a terribly poor country, just barely staying alive? They wouldn't think, "science took away my God but gave me a lot in return." They have nothing on Earth, and if this world is all there is, they are left in despair.

Agnes: I have no idea if giving up God would make most people depressed. I also wonder if having a severe physical or mental illness would increase the importance of belief. And does belief ease the suffering of starving desert nomads, or would they be miserable regardless of their religion?

Althea: No doubt faith makes some folks happier, at least in the short run, but people are remarkably resilient. Besides, happiness is strongly influenced by brain function and biochemistry. There are lots of clinically depressed believers and skeptics with sunny dispositions.[161] And atheists who go through emotionally difficult periods often feel renewed affirmation from within. I recall a comment by Albert Camus: "In the midst of winter I found within myself an invincible spring."

Think back to the way you experienced this dialogue. Which statements made you think, *"That's right"*? Which claims seemed fallacious? Which comments made you squirm? Did you tend to focus on statements you agree with? Did it feel good to validate your own opinions by hanging on to those arguments?

You can see why I keep asking questions such as these. If we want to understand other viewpoints, we need to pay attention to ideas that push against our preconceptions. Of course, reading these dialogues may help you articulate your own reasons for believing as you do. That's certainly useful, but you can also s t r e t c h yourself toward a deeper appreciation of other perspectives.

Is Religion Bad for Us?

Some people lose their faith because they are sickened by the wickedness of religious organizations. History books show church leaders burning heretics alive, stirring up witch-hunts, and fomenting "holy" wars. Unfortunately, religion is still fanning the flames of inter-group conflict today. Let's tune in again to our trialogue.

Althea: One reason I'm an atheist is that religion undermines morality. I am appalled, for example, that the most grotesquely disturbing accounts of torture I have ever read involve techniques perfected during the Spanish Inquisition.[162] Christian torturers went to fiendish extremes with the full approval of the church. This contradicts the idea that piety makes us loving.

Theodore: Althea, I once heard a preacher say that the church is the only organization in the world *for sinners only.* If you never sin, why go to church? We need churches, temples, mosques, ashrams, and synagogues because they can help us become better people. But since human beings are in charge of religious institutions, they will sometimes pervert religion for terrible purposes.

Althea: I want to read a few things that tie in here, first from *The End of Faith.* Sam Harris says the problem is religion itself, even so-called moderate religion. Each religion teaches its followers that other faith traditions are "at best, dangerously incomplete." So every creed is intolerant at its core! Harris also charges that religious moderates help cause strife, "because their beliefs provide the context in which scriptural literalism and religious violence can never be adequately opposed."[163]

Theodore: You know that I think Harris goes off the deep end. Many Christians respect other faith traditions. Besides, even if Harris is exactly right about religion, his argument has nothing to do with rejecting God. Maybe all the major religions have botched their job, distorting the divine revelations they have received.

Althea: A psychologist of religion named David Wulff has found a correlation between church membership and "ethnocentrism, authoritarianism, dogmatism, social distance, rigidity, intolerance of ambiguity, and specific forms of prejudice, especially against Jews and blacks."[164] Think of that! The more religious you are, the more rigid and prejudiced you are likely to be. Scotty McLennan offers "evidence that religion is itself a root cause of conflict and violence." In giving us a sense of identity, it divides us into in-groups and out-groups.[165] Remember the Thirty Years' War in the 1600s? It was partly a war between religious groups and it killed *one-third* of the population in large areas of Europe, even with the crude armaments they had at the time.[166] So religion often intensifies people's viciousness instead of reforming them. And here's how this ties into belief in God. If religious people were really relating to an all-powerful, all-good supreme being that wanted to fill their hearts with love and compassion, wouldn't this typically make them better instead of worse? But they aren't getting better, because they are not tapping into anything grand and transcendent. They're only relating to their own fantasies.

Theodore: Not all atheists are sure that religion is bad for us. Daniel Dennett acknowledges that "for day-in, day-out lifelong bracing, there is probably nothing so effective as religion: it makes powerful and talented people more humble and patient, it makes average people rise above themselves, it provides sturdy support for many people who desperately need help staying away from drink or drugs or crime."[167]

Althea: Dennett ends up saying he is not sure whether religion is mostly helpful or harmful. He sees that with something as multi-faceted as religion you can't just add up the good and bad as if you were filling in a financial ledger. That's a fair point. But if religious people were in touch with a supreme goodness, they would tend to be morally superior to us "heathens." Nobel Laureate Steven Weinberg's comment rings true: Without religion "you would have good people doing good things and evil people doing evil things. But for good people to do evil things, that takes religion."

Agnes: I feel like I'm watching ping-pong.

Theodore: And it's my serve. Going back to religious wars, let's remember that people tend to be tribal. In *The Philosophical Baby,* Alison Gopnik talks about how easy it is for people to dehumanize members of an out-group, even if they are divided into groups arbitrarily. Have some people wear red feathers and others blue feathers, and "very quickly the red feathers will start to prefer the company of other red feathers and decide that the blue feathers just aren't their type. You don't need a long history of conflict or oppression to hate another group. Just giving them a different name is enough."[168] Religion cannot always overcome such a powerful human tendency.

Althea: So if we were created in God's image, how come we have this built-in design defect? Also, some say that God must exist because so many people testify that they are in contact with a supreme being. But if churchgoers show no evidence that their spiritual life is making them better persons, how can we give their testimony any credence? Suppose I say, "Hey, Theodore, did you know that I exercise every day in an invisible gymnasium in my living room?" Even if I managed to convince you that a gym could be invisible, wouldn't you be skeptical of my claim if you noticed that I was getting weaker instead of stronger?

Theodore: Not so fast, Althea. Robin Gill has a whole book indicating that churchgoers behave better than those who don't attend services.[169] I think it's obvious that belief in God keeps a lot of us on the straight and narrow. It definitely helps me curb my selfishness and irritability.

Althea: Actually Gill's book suggests that Christians and non-Christians behave similarly in most respects.

Agnes: OK, you two, how about we declare a truce? I agree with Dennett that it's hard to say whether religion in general is making people better or worse. Although you can't prove God by saying, "look how much good religion does for people," you can't disprove God by showing that religion makes them nasty. Maybe people have just enough religion to make them hate, but not enough to make them love.

            ❧ ❧ ❧ ❧ ❧ ❧ ❧ ❧ ❧ ❧ ❧ ❧ ❧ ❧

Recall your own thoughts about these issues. When you think about religion (either in general or your own faith tradition), how has it helped the world and how has it hurt?

We'll give our three friends a break and come back to them in Chapter Eleven.

Before going on, some personal comments: While I appreciate the open-minded, kind-hearted people I have met at interfaith gatherings, I see some truth in Sam Harris' critique of moderation. Moderate believers inadvertently provide "cover" for vicious zealots, who love to claim the legitimacy of belonging to a great spiritual tradition. If you are on the side of love, it's time to stand up to the haters. That doesn't mean hating them in turn, but it does mean speaking out vigorously against religious bigotry.

Is "Faith" Destructive?

Some religions stress the importance of faith, and non-believers criticize this emphasis. Sam Harris sees faith as harmful, if it means "*unjustified* belief in matters of ultimate concern . . . ."[170] For Richard Dawkins, faith is "an evil precisely because it requires no justification and brooks no argument."[171] But let's be careful here. Faith is an "octopus word" with several distinct meanings. In discussing faith with friends or loved ones, it's easy to talk right past each other.

Here are two ways of thinking about religious faith:

A. Faith is strong belief without strong evidence.
B. Faith is wholehearted commitment.

In Option A, belief is not primarily based upon evidence. At times it is based on manipulation, so that people are cajoled, bullied, shamed, or brainwashed into having faith. Some churches even say it's sinful to ask for evidence.[172] If we don't use reason and evidence, we will probably fall back on tradition and authority, and this could justify any belief-system.

Unfortunately religion has a long history of affirming faith in ways that devalue reason. In the 1500s, Martin Luther claimed that

"Reason should be destroyed in all Christians"[173] and "a Christian should tear the eyes out of his reason."[174]

American political leader William Jennings Bryan seems to have taken Luther's counsel to heart: "If the Bible had said that Jonah swallowed the whale, I would believe it." And, "If we have to give up either religion or education, we should give up education."[175]

Sometimes, then, faith can mean strong belief without strong evidence. Let's turn now to option B, faith as wholehearted commitment. Certain theologians, such as John Haught, view faith as "the commitment of one's whole being to God." It is a "self-surrender in which one's whole being, and not just the intellect, is experienced as being carried away into a dimension of reality that is much deeper and more real than anything that could be grasped by science and reason."[176]

Although atheists might think of "being carried away" as rather passive and unreflective, I doubt that this is what Haught has in mind. A skeptic might also quarrel with Haught's quotation from Holmes Rolston III that "there is no knowing without going."[177] This seems to mean that we cannot know whether God exists unless we surrender to the experience of deity, but atheists could turn the tables and use this suggestion to their advantage. After abandoning belief in God, some atheists have insights which never occurred to them as believers. They might conclude that we cannot transcend illusion without delving into our doubts, putting a secular twist on "no knowing without going."

There is, however, an important kernel of truth in "no knowing without going." We cannot achieve profound wisdom on the cheap. Deep mysteries demand in-depth exploration. But to have confidence in any belief-system, we need to carefully consider the alternatives. One could thoroughly explore belief in a supreme being, and also "test drive" non-belief, sincerely and courageously. A more complete understanding would require other investigations as well.

Realistically, few of us will take the time to do all that. But if we only investigate one set of possibilities, we cannot know that our beliefs are well-founded. That would be like saying, "This is the greatest country in the world! And I won't waste my time visiting other places to see what they are like." If we have not walked for many miles in the shoes of a theist, or an atheist, we should refrain from harshly criticizing that person's belief-system.

So faith can involve Option A (faith is belief without strong evidence) or Option B (faith is wholehearted commitment). Many atheists and agnostics could support Option B if it explicitly affirmed the value of reason: *Faith is hope and trust which build upon evidence.* Importantly, this sort of faith can use the power of honest doubt to test and refine religious convictions.

Look back over this discussion of faith. What was interesting, helpful, or surprising? What does faith mean in your own life? What would you like it to mean in the future?

Summing up: For many people, theism is so much more appealing than atheism that they have little interest in questioning God's existence. To others, the secular lifestance feels just fine.

Some non-believers say the influence of religion is mainly negative. They maintain that if religion really puts people in touch with a loving super-intelligence, believers would be more consistently caring and compassionate. Most theists, however, feel that belief does help them live good lives.

Faith can mean a number of things, including strong belief without strong evidence and belief as wholehearted commitment. Those who are critical of religion emphasize that commitments should be anchored in reliable evidence.

Beware of all-or-nothing claims that we're doomed to despair without religion or that religious belief is the root of all evil. People can make meaning and find value through all sorts of world-views, drawing strength from a well-grounded spiritual or secular faith in which evidence, trust, and hope are woven together.

Chapter Ten
God and Morality

As we saw earlier, people have so closely connected atheism with sinfulness that some dictionaries have defined "atheist" as a person who lives immorally. Many would agree with Dinesh D'Souza that "If you kill God, morality also dies. You can't cut the roots and keep the branches."[178]

Can We Be Good Without God?

The current Pope certainly thinks we need God to be good. Although the Roman Catholic Church now respects the legitimacy of other religions, it still condemns secularism. On July 7, 2009, Pope Benedict XVI's encyclical, *Caritas in Veritate,* asserted that "When nature, including the human being, is viewed as the result of mere chance or evolutionary determinism, our sense of responsibility wanes."[179]

The Rev. Rick Warren expresses similar sentiments in *The Purpose-Driven Life,* one of the best-selling books in the history of publishing: "If your time on earth were all there is to your life, I would suggest you start living it up immediately. You could forget about being good and ethical, and you wouldn't have to worry about any consequences of your actions. You could indulge yourself in total self-centeredness because your actions would have no long-term repercussions."[180] (Here "long-term" means for all eternity.)

I was shocked by this passage, and I wondered whether Warren actually believes this claim. Notice that when he says there would be "no long-term repercussions" of a person's actions, he means no repercussions *for that person.* Obviously what we do (and don't do) has repercussions beyond our own little lives, just as stones tossed in a lake make ever-widening ripples. His message is that if we were not afraid of being punished after we die, then the best course of action, the strategy which he himself would *suggest,* would be to throw morality into the trash can. Our guiding principle would become "total self-centeredness."

I don't think Rev. Warren is joking. He actually seems to assume that the only reason we would want to be good is that we will be punished if we're bad. Without this threat, our selfishness would be total. But I doubt that this is true of people in general or Rick Warren in particular. Warren does a lot of wonderful things, and I suspect that he truly *wants* to do many of his good works, regardless of whether these good deeds buy him a ticket to heaven. Furthermore, his pessimistic view of human nature contradicts the teaching that we are made in the image of God. And how can anyone who observes the dedication of parents caring for their children see humans as totally selfish?

I will need to defend atheism in this chapter, not to prove its correctness but just to show that it's a non-disastrous alternative. If most of those who do not fear God's wrath become immoral, that would be disastrous indeed. Fortunately, it just isn't so.

Daniel Dennett has found no indication that those who do not believe in divine reward and punishment "are more likely to kill, rape, rob, or break their promises than people who do." Dennett is an atheist, so he does have a horse in this race, but he cites compelling data. American prisons include Christians, Jews, Muslims, and the non-religious, "represented about as they are in the general population." He even cites evidence that unbelievers "have the lowest divorce rate in the United States, and born-again Christians the highest."[181]

Benjamin Beit-Hallahmi goes further: "The claim that atheists are somehow likely to be immoral or dishonest has long been disproven by systematic studies. In studies that looked at readiness to help or honesty, it was atheists that distinguished themselves, not the religious . . . ." He also notes that "ever since the field of criminology got started . . . the fact that the unaffiliated and the nonreligious had the lowest crime rates has been noted . . . ."[182]

William Murry points out that people had moral impulses long before the Ten Commandments. "Versions of the Golden Rule arose in several ancient cultures, including those in which theism was either weak or absent." He also reports the finding of political scientist James Q. Wilson that every society believes it is wrong to lie, commit murder or incest, and break promises, and all cultures value family loyalty and taking care of children.[183] This suggests that some aspects of morality are built into human nature. In fact, recent studies of infants and toddlers show that moral sensitivities appear early in life. Even two-year-olds distinguish between breaking rules and hurting someone. They see both rule-breaking and hurting people as bad, but they consider hurting people to be much worse than breaking a rule.[184] Two-year-olds! This study and many others[185] contradicts the claim that humans are totally egocentric.

A theist could reply that our moral sense is fragile, often overpowered by selfishness or culturally-backed cruelty. Belief in God may strengthen our weak and inconsistent ethical aspirations.

Although we could abandon belief in God without throwing out morality, the transition from personal theism to naturalism might be troublesome. Any major revision of the way we understand ethics could tempt us to rationalize shallow and selfish behavior. At the same time, some of the most secular nations, "such as those in Scandinavia, are among the least violent, best educated, and most likely to care for the poor."[186] So in at least some places, a societal transition toward secular humanism seems to be going well.

Did God Create Right and Wrong?

Regardless of whether religion improves our behavior, some say we need a supreme being to establish any sort of morality at all. It is God who constitutes some things as good and some things as evil. Ivan in *The Brothers Karamazov* is often quoted as saying that without God, "everything is permitted." In his book-length reflection on agnosticism, Michael Krasny ponders Ivan's comment, "searching . . . for something that could give moral force to the choice of doing good, something that could [replace] the moral hegemony and moral power of God."[187]

Saying that God decides what is good and evil fits the *divine command theory* of ethics. God determines right and wrong. If God says humans have worth, then we do. If not, we're worthless. If God says killing people is bad, we must prohibit murder. If God says killing is good, we must promote it. Whoever dealt the cards gets to make the rules.

Plato considered this idea thousands of years ago. In a famous dialogue he has Socrates ask, "Do the gods love good things because they are good, or are good things good because the gods love them?"[188] But the seventeenth-century philosopher Gottfried Wilhelm Leibniz spotted a gaping hole in the divine command theory. If one says "that things are good not because they match up to objective standards of goodness, but only because God chose them, you will unthinkingly destroy all God's love and all his glory. For why praise him for what he has done, if he would be equally praiseworthy for doing just the opposite?"[189]

There is a story about two theological students who were arguing vehemently, late into the night, about the nature of deity. Finally one of them exclaimed, "Oh, now I see! My god is your devil and your devil is my god."

Think about that. Who decides which invisible spirit should be *called* a god and which one should be called a devil? In general, "god" means a great supernatural power that we humans label as good and "devil" means a supernatural power we label as bad. Morality comes first. Everything and everyone must be judged by the standard of the highest values. Even God is thus accountable.[190]

The Threat of Moral Relativism

If morality is not established by God, then what does establish it? Is there an independent standard of goodness? And how would we gain access to this standard? Is it written in the sky?

Perhaps there is no independent, objective standard that is "true" in the same sense that it is true that birds have beaks and Boston is north of Atlanta. Perhaps the basic principles of right and wrong, good and evil, are *judgments* about what is positive and what is negative. For example, we humans judge intense and unending pain to be bad, and we usually judge happiness to be good.

This way of looking at right and wrong involves a sort of moral relativism. Although this term can mean several different things, I'm talking about the idea that good and evil are *relative* to the moral standards of someone who makes moral judgments. People can make such judgments. So could a personal god or an intelligent space alien. All opinions about good and evil must be based on the standards of some moral evaluator.

If good and evil, right and wrong, are judgments instead of discoveries about facts, can we cook up any moral system that strikes our fancy? Not at all. Even when we make core value-judgments ourselves rather than learning them from others, we do not make such judgments capriciously. They well up from the very center of our being. By comparison, think about how we experience music. When lovely music overwhelms us with emotion, it calls forth a deep personal response. I cannot arbitrarily decide that the next song that plays on the radio will seem to be the loveliest I have ever heard. Nor can I decide that from this day forward I will find it morally praiseworthy to torment goldfish.

Moral relativism presents significant challenges, because we do not all agree about bedrock value-judgments. Does belief in God help solve this problem?

If God created us, our creator would presumably know more than we do about the values and ethical principles that are best suited for humans. But people of different religions (and even the same religion) understand the will of God in very different ways. We have no independent and objective standard for deciding who is correct. Often when people say "God wants this," they are merely expressing their own biases. *"Thus saith the Lord"* sounds more impressive than *"Thus saith me,"* but it may amount to the same thing. So regardless of whether you are a theist, an atheist, or an agnostic, moral relativism is an important issue. Fortunately there is a lot of overlap among competing value-systems. Humanity could greatly benefit if we did a better job of focusing on the values most of us have in common. If we did that well, this could be a wonderful world.[191]

The Problem of Evil

In thinking about the relationship between God and goodness, theologians struggle to combine these three ideas:

(1) God is omnipotent (all-powerful).
(2) God is perfectly loving and just.
(3) Evil exists.

It is notoriously difficult to reconcile God's love and power with countless tragedies in the lives of living creatures. Perhaps God refrains from using all available power in order to leave room for human freedom. But this does not address the dreadful suffering that results from God's creating animals that can only survive by killing and eating other animals. Theodicy, the attempt to solve the problem of evil, tends to ignore non-human creatures or assume that they have little value.

Atheists can also point out that according to the Bible, God directly caused terrible tragedies. For instance, after getting upset about human sinfulness, God decided to kill almost all living creatures by drowning them in a flood. To atheists that sounds about as appropriate as using a nuclear weapon to annihilate a gnat. Even if Noah's flood never occurred, scientists say there have been several mass extinctions, including one which wiped out over 90% of all species.[192] This was millions of years before humans even existed. If animals have value and their suffering matters, what was the point of all this destruction?

One way to approach the problem of evil is to say that it's a mystery. Perhaps we are simply incapable of understanding why evil pervades our world. Even though this might be correct, it seems like a dangerous idea. Saying we should overlook a seemingly enormous theological problem because there may be some solution we cannot grasp could lead us to rationalize just about any belief system.

I want to share a story told by my friend Will Cloughley about the tension between belief in God and the existence of radical evil. Will writes:

"In my young mind, God was not an intellectual proposition. God was the assurance that in spite of mishaps and troubles, everything in the end would be OK. He was the answer to the Nameless Dread and the unfathomable darkness." In early adulthood, on a ship bound for Europe, Will read *The Diary of Anne Frank*. "I distinctly remember the moment I read that Anne – naked, cold, starving, and lice-ridden – had finally succumbed to typhus in a Nazi concentration camp, her body thrown into a mass grave. I put the book down, left the cabin, and fled toward the bow of the ship which was enclosed by a circular railing. And from that pulpit at the prow I actually shook my fist at the open sky as Job of old might have done and shouted in a hoarse voice, 'Why? Why? Why?'

"My shout expressed my outrage and grief – not only for Anne, but for the many innocents who shared her fate in a world that was too dark and grim to imagine that there was anything like an omnipotent and loving God.

"It was then that something remarkable happened. The surface of the water to the right and left of the ship shivered as several hundred flying fish lifted into a long glide as if they were a flock of birds. Then they plunged back into the water only to re-emerge some seconds later for another long glide. I had never seen or heard of flying fish before. I intuitively felt their flight as an expression of some primal exuberance, perhaps the same qualities that in their ancestors had directed their evolution toward this daring reach into another dimension.

"The coincidental juncture of these two experiences transmuted my emotions in a way that is difficult to explain and could be thought of as having the qualities of a Zen *koan*. It was as if I had gone to a Zen teacher and asked, 'Master, why did God allow a great evil to take the life of young Anne Frank?' And the answer was, 'Flying fish.'"[193]

Will's story provides no philosophical explanation for radical evil, but I found myself moved by this juxtaposition of human grief and natural beauty. A healing response to our anguished cry of "Why? Why?" sometimes comes in the most unlikely ways and places.

Alternatives to Omnipotence

The claim that God is omnipotent is supported by the testimony of some religious visionaries, who say they have directly experienced the fact that God is all-powerful. But how does one experience such a thing? Perhaps a thunderous voice proclaimed, "I am the Lord, and I hereby inform you that I am 'omnipotent' in the standard theological sense of that term." In most cases, however, I suspect that visionaries have simply *felt* an overwhelming power that staggered their imaginations. This led them to say that God is omnipotent, but they could easily have reached a more modest conclusion: God is far, far more powerful than anything else we know. How could one tell the difference between encountering absolute power and encountering power that is merely mind-boggling?

The problem of evil can be ameliorated by denying God's omnipotence, but some think this solution carries too great a cost. To say that the creator of the universe cannot prevent evil might shake people's faith. In praying to a deity whose power is limited, they could never be sure of receiving adequate assistance. On the other hand, even if God has limitless power, we cannot know whether our prayers will be answered as we would wish. An omnipotent being is still constrained in various ways. For instance, it is impossible for an infinitely good being to choose to do anything less than the best. Sometimes doing what's best means allowing bad things to happen because they will lead to a greater good. Christians certainly do not see it as "good" that Jesus died in agony, but they believe that his suffering led to (or was in some way closely connected with) our salvation.

In short, even if God is *able* to do anything, God's choices about how to *use* this ability may be limited by factors beyond our understanding. Thus it might make little practical difference to believers if God is seen as extremely powerful rather than all-powerful. This would ease the problem of evil considerably.

Another, more radical approach, challenges the whole notion that the highest power is coercive power, the dominance of one force over another. Many respected religious teachers advocate *process theology,* which celebrates the persuasive, encouraging, inspirational power of God. Christian process thinkers such as John B. Cobb, Jr. see this liberating power revealed in the life of Jesus Christ. Citing extensive scholarly evidence, Cobb maintains that the idea of omnipotence was never emphasized in either Hebrew or Christian scriptures. Passages referring to "God almighty" actually mistranslate the ancient word *shaddai.*[194]

While brute force is impressive in the short run, many theologians contend that the highest power is love rather than compulsion. Without divine compulsion bad things can and do happen, but process theologians would prefer this sort of cosmos to one in which a supreme super-controller orchestrated every movement of every molecule, every single second.

Summing up: Although atheism has been associated with sinfulness, many unbelievers live exemplary lives. Cross-cultural studies and studies of infants and children suggest that we are born with an innate moral sense.

If we could agree about what God wants us to do, that could help us deal with moral relativism, but such agreement eludes us.

One way to solve the problem of evil is to say that God's power may "only" be astonishing rather than entirely unlimited.

Chapter Eleven
God and Mortality

People want to believe in God to ease their fear of death, and evidence of immortality[195] helps support theistic faith.

Evidence of an afterlife is abundant – near-death experiences, memories of past lives, out-of-body episodes, ghost sightings, visions of departed loved ones, and channeled communications from the great beyond. The quality of this evidence is variable. Many atheists and agnostics (and some theists) deny that any of it is sound.

Evaluating research about life after death is beyond the scope of this book. I tend to be skeptical of reports of paranormal phenomena, such as traveling away from one's body and being visited by spirits, but I admit that afterlife-related data has impressed many scholars, including some atheists.

I should also acknowledge another strong opinion: After we die I do not think any of us will spend eternity in hell. To me, the concept of hell reflects the all-too-human tendency to divide the world into good guys and bad guys. Obviously many readers will disagree with me about that, and, as always, I hope you will take whatever works for you and leave the rest.

For a controversial new Christian critique of the doctrine of hell, see *Love Wins: A Book About Heaven, Hell, and the Fate of Every Person Who Ever Lived*, by Rob Bell.

At the End of a Loved One's Life

Believers and non-believers who love each other confront special challenges when one of them becomes terminally ill. A husband, for example, may see his wife's pending death as the end of her existence, while she hopes to wake up in heaven. She, in turn, may wonder if they will ever meet again, fearing that her spouse is destined for a noticeably warmer location.

I will offer ways of dealing with two possible scenarios, but these are exquisitely difficult situations and we should not expect perfect solutions.

First scenario: *You are a theist and you worry that a terminally ill loved one will go to hell.* Here is a way of looking at this issue that is compatible with most mainstream religions: We know little for certain about what happens after death, but we can count on God to do what is loving and just. When we finally see how the troubles and limitations of Earthly life are resolved by divine providence, we will be filled with joy. We can trust that all will be well, even though we do not fully understand God's plan of salvation.

Second scenario: *You are an atheist. Your dying spouse (parent, child, etc.) believes eternity awaits, whereas you feel you are saying goodbye forever.* Obviously this isn't the best time to persuade someone to doubt his or her theological convictions. Instead, you could convey a loving and magnanimous message: "Right now I actually hope I am wrong about religion. I want you to live forever, and I want to be with you always. I am happy for you to do whatever will help you draw strength from your faith." You can emphasize how precious your time together has been, and how memories will comfort you in spite of your grief. "I would feel great sadness in losing you even if I was a religious person. In these final weeks I just want to be close, feeling our love for each other till the last."

That concluding statement may be the most important, because theists, atheists and agnostics can all agree on the power and value of love. Express your love in words, show it in actions, share it as a caress.

So these are some thoughts about a particularly vexing situation. I would appreciate hearing from readers who can offer ideas or stories about how couples with different philosophies of life face terminal illness.

To further explore end-of-life issues, let's hear from Theodore, Althea, and Agnes.

A Dialogue About Death

Agnes: I sometimes lean toward believing in God for frankly selfish reasons. I want to live on after my body fades into oblivion, and religion promises me that God will raise us from the dead. It sounds unlikely, but it could be true.

Althea: Unlikely indeed! Freud was right to call eternal life a wish-fulfillment fantasy. To soothe our fear of death we imagine floating off into a celestial retirement community where everyone signs up for harp lessons. But even those who say they believe in an afterlife dread the grim reaper. There's an old saying: "Everybody wants to go to heaven but nobody wants to die."

Theodore: Althea, my faith in immortality eases my fears considerably. And maybe you've heard *this* old saying: "There are no atheists in foxholes."

Althea: People intend that wisecrack as a slam against atheism, but if it were true it would poke a huge hole in the case for theism. It would mean that the fundamental reason people believe in God is that they're scared not to! Their fear of death overwhelms all other considerations. To the extent that this is actually so, no one can be confident that a supreme being exists. Those who are afraid to doubt God's reality can never know whether their faith is well-founded. They cannot tell whether they believe for sound reasons, or just to allay their own anxieties.

Theodore: OK, Althea, I admit that the foxholes joke[196] is a cheap shot.

Althea: One fellow who thought Christians believe in God because they are scared of death was the philosopher Arthur

Schopenhauer. And Schopenhauer pulled a brilliant reverse move, saying that if an afterlife could "be proved to be incompatible with the existence of gods, . . . they would soon sacrifice these gods to their own immortality, and be eager for atheism."[197]

Theodore: But going back to the main issue, the evidence that God exists and the evidence that we live on after death are complimentary. They support each other. I have confidence that eternal life is a reality, and this belief fits religious teachings from all over the world. People's experiences of a supreme goodness with ultimate power imply that God will care for everything that is precious. If I want to protect something I value and I have the power to protect it, then I *will* protect it. If I can be relied on in this way, so can my maker. I cannot believe a creator would produce such amazing beings as humans and then just throw them in the trash.

Althea: But he would throw them into hell!

Theodore: Althea, don't assume you know all my beliefs just because you know I'm a Christian. To me, hell is a symbolic way of talking about what it's like to be alienated from God. I don't take it literally, and I don't know that being in hell needs to last forever. I have never pretended to completely understand heaven, hell, sin, and salvation. Cartoon-pictures of demons with pitchforks tormenting sinners seem juvenile. But I trust that whatever happens will express both absolute love and total justice.

Althea: I guess I thought it was my turn to take a cheap shot. If you don't believe God tortures people forever, I'm glad to hear that. As you know, I'm not impressed by data on near-death experiences and so on. But even if there is an afterlife, it could occur without God. Remember, some atheists believe in reincarnation.

Agnes: How would that work without God?

Althea: I have no idea, but we have no idea how to explain lots of phenomena that are much better documented than reincarnation.

Theodore: Most data on the afterlife makes it sound wonderful, much more fulfilling than life on Earth. This is one common theme in near-death experiences, and it supports the Christian idea that what awaits us is a far better world than we can even imagine.

Althea: On the other hand a lot of theists doubt or disbelieve in life after death. Karen Armstrong does not think most religions emphasize immortality, and she herself is completely agnostic about this issue.[198] She also pointed out that religion is supposed to be about transcending our egos, not ensuring our own survival.

Agnes: Anthony Freeman mentions Buddhism's emphasis on accepting "our fleetingness, our nothingness, our need to 'embrace the void.'" He mentions research showing that many Christians who regularly attend church "do not believe in life after death."[199]

Theodore: Since we're quoting religious writers I'll play another card. The priest and paleontologist, Teilhard de Chardin, wrote, "The prospect of a *total death* (and that is a word to which we should devote much thought if we are to gauge its destructive effect on our souls) will, I warn you, when it has become part of our consciousness, immediately dry up in us the springs from which our efforts are drawn."[200]

Althea: So if we don't get to live forever we'll all shrivel up and suck our thumbs, quivering with terror? Ridiculous! What Mark Twain said rings true for me: "I do not fear death. I had been dead for billions and billions of years before I was born, and had not suffered the slightest inconvenience from it."

Agnes: The prospect of being dead for billions of years in the future is disturbing, but we are "missing" just as much life because of not having been alive for billions in the past. Even so, I wonder how Mr. Twain actually felt on his deathbed. Maybe it seemed just a smidge "inconvenient" when extinction was staring him right in the face.

Althea: Lots of atheists meet death without shaking in their boots. For example, one elderly woman said that she "took comfort from knowing that the fragments of which she was made, when she died, would . . . be resolved into the universe – the ever wonderful universe – from which they had come. The one-ness of herself would go back into a greater one-ness, too grand for the grandest dream to begin to fathom . . . ."[201]

Agnes: I realize that my worry about eternal life may reflect spiritual immaturity. I have already lived long enough to have had all sorts of satisfying experiences. How many more do I need? I can relate to Susan Ertz's comment that "Millions long for immortality who don't know what to do with themselves on a rainy Sunday afternoon."

Theodore: We do seem to have an unlimited desire for more, more, more.

Agnes: However some people don't want to go on forever. Paul Tillich, a Christian, thought that an endless afterlife would be hell, and many agree with him.[202] In fact the ultimate goal of some religions is to free us from an endless cycle of rebirths. That's all well and good, but I'm still rather fond of perpetual existence.

Theodore: James P. Carse seems to agree with Tillich. He speculates that endless personal consciousness would drive us mad with boredom.[203] He also backs up Armstrong's suggestion that ancient religions did not focus on eternal life.[204] But I do not agree. Folklore all over the world speaks of visitations from the dead. Most people in most cultures have assumed that we do go on in some form. The Bible would not have announced the afterlife as an astonishing revelation. It was taken for granted by most everyone.

Agnes: Very true. When preliterate people had dreams of dead companions, this seemed to confirm that personal reality persists beyond the grave. Immortality has always been our default assumption. People have mostly been worried about what our future existence will be like, not whether we will continue. Today, however, many fear that death will be the end.

Theodore: But yearning for an afterlife is not just about saving our own dear little hides. We want our loved ones to keep on living, and we want loving communities of friends and family to endure. We want justice, but the world is full of injustice. And we want meaning, which is threatened by oblivion. All of this just cries out for a world beyond this one.

Agnes: The end of life also radically disrupts our plans, projects, and personal connections. If we walked around focusing on the fact that our mortal lives (or even the entire Earth) could vanish at any second, that would be unnerving to say the least. I want so much for life to go on, but does it?

Althea: People try to fix all the problems of this world by kicking them upstairs into heaven. I know that sounded flip, and I do understand the desire to have everything come out all right. But folks, I just don't think it works. If someone goes though awful experiences on Earth, those are not erased by making it all better later on. As far as personal survival goes, I would prefer to keep living. I have an inborn survival instinct. And yet I am absolutely sure that being alive long enough to feel love and wonder is far better than never living at all.

Theodore: Of course.

Agnes: It seems to me that many people are cushioned from the full brunt of their own mortality, because it is so difficult to imagine actually ceasing to be. This sort of denial makes it easier for soldiers to rush into combat and for rock climbers to crawl up sheer cliffs – which is good in some ways and bad in others. So our psychological makeup softens the fear of dying. I wish that worked better for me.

Althea: On the other hand, because it is hard to imagine totally disappearing, we may think of death as if it were a terribly unpleasant combination of existing and not existing. Because we won't exist, we think of blackness, emptiness, and total silence. But we half-imagine ourselves experiencing these frightening things, missing our old bodily incarnation. I also think people dread eternal nothingness out of a vague sense that it would be awful to be nonexistent for so long. But only creatures that exist can feel awful about anything.

Agnes: If death-as-extinction does happen, we won't be there to feel bad about that. *All we will ever know is life, so we will never "be" dead*. Death will not and cannot touch us.[205] The main problem here is not death, but rather my fear of death.

Althea: Even though I'd like to live forever (or maybe a million years would do), there is real value in knowing "this is it!" As Emily Dickenson wrote, "That it will never come again / Is what makes life so sweet."[206] And if we realized that we only have a few decades, years, or even days to show people that we love them, we might stop putting it off till tomorrow. In fact, thinking of life's brevity sometimes leaves me feeling uplifted. Not always! But it does help me focus on living fully today. Remembering that I will come to an end shines a spotlight on *right-here-now*. Each moment becomes more brilliant, by contrast to the non-light of not-being. In that way I do think that death illuminates life.

ɛ₰ ɛ₰ ɛ₰ ɛ₰ ɛ₰ ɛ₰ ɛ₰ ɛ₰ ɛ₰ ɛ₰ ɛ₰ ɛ₰ ɛ₰ ɛ₰

Speaking Personally

In writing this chapter I have felt biases which pull me in opposite directions. On the one hand, I have a strong desire for personal continuity and I would like to know that we will survive the grave. However I do not count on this outcome, and I think Buddhists may be right in challenging us to let go of craving permanence in a world of constant flux.

I have been impressed by several parishioners who were not intensely attached to their own persistence, elderly men and women who accepted life's ending graciously even though they did not expect an afterlife. In particular I think of Marilyn MacIntyre, of Orange Coast Unitarian Universalist Church in Costa Mesa, California. One day Marilyn confided to me that she had Lou Gehrig's disease, with just a year or two to live. During her final months she told me, "If you can accept life, you can accept death with it. It is all part of the same thing. I don't know what will come after I die. Whatever it is, it's the natural thing, and that's okay." I believe Marilyn faced death courageously when her life reached its end.

And then there's Frank Powell. Frank was the father of Jean Brookhart, also a member of Orange Coast Church. Jean suspected that her dad was an agnostic. He was a dedicated humanitarian who founded the first bureau for handicapped children in Wisconsin, and set up programs for youngsters with hearing problems, rheumatic heart trouble, and other ailments. When at last he was on his deathbed a local minister came by and asked him, "Frank, have you made your peace with God?" Echoing the words of Henry David Thoreau, the old man replied, "As far as I know, I have not quarreled with him." "Well then," said the pastor, "are you confident that your soul will attain salvation?" "Reverend, I've spent my life up to this point thinking about other people and I'm not going to start worrying about myself now."

At the funeral, the minister said he had to respect a man who could give those answers.

Another elder inspired me by sending the gift of his words. Ministers sometimes receive books in the mail that authors hope they will mention to their congregations. About 20 years ago a slim volume arrived called *Light, Love and Life,* by Edwin A. Burtt. His name was familiar, and he had written a text I read in college, *The Teachings of the Compassionate Buddha.* Burtt taught at Cornell from 1932 till 1960. His message was arresting:

"Soon after I had reached the age of eighty I made a provocative discovery about myself. . . . I had not learned how to live. . . . To realize this truth was quite a shock. I was over eighty years old and steadily getting older. . . . Could one learn to live at such an age?"

"So, at eighty, my strenuous searching began." In *Light, Love and Life,* Burtt shares many uplifting discoveries, including comments he made after age ninety about how to find joy when death is drawing near: "If one has learned how to live, even though very incompletely, one can live more cheerfully and hopefully in old age than at any earlier time."

The key is to dedicate oneself to higher values. "If one has given himself before death to those values, what can death do to him?" Such dedication moves one "from the self-centeredness that inevitably perishes to the outflowing responsiveness that is the earmark of vigorous life. . . . It may be that the best way to make old age a fully satisfying part of life is to let the temporal self die by the time old age comes – that is, to shift the center of selfhood to a reality beyond the obviously mortal body." Thus we can expand "into a more capacious self which has left its previous boundary behind. . . . To love is by its very nature to become united with a reality outside of and more enduring than one's body. . . . however intensely an egotist may crave survival, all that he cares for is obviously transitory. 'Love or Perish' becomes an inescapable challenge."

Burtt also shares a wonderful way of re-conceptualizing eternal life: *"Not where I breathe, but where I love, I am."*[207]

I hope atheists and agnostics can appreciate the fact that religious belief comforts those who mourn and allays the dread of personal cessation. I hope theists can acknowledge that many non-believers cope well with mortality. Some are serene, taking death as part of life. And even those who earnestly wish they could continue may find fulfillment in experiences that are limited in time but limitless in value. As Robert Frost wrote, "Happiness makes up in height what it lacks in length."

Summing up: The fear of mortality motivates faith in God, and evidence of immortality supports theism. Certain religious experiences seem to reveal a supreme goodness that values us, wants to protect us, and has the power to do so.

Some people dislike the idea of going on forever, and some religions encourage us to let go of craving endless survival.

We can expand our sense of self to include what lives on when we are gone: "Not where I breathe, but where I love, I am."[208]

In the book's concluding chapters we will consider the potential benefits of an open-minded, open-hearted approach to religious differences, and how we can continue to deepen these benefits.

THE ROAD AHEAD

Chapters Twelve, Thirteen, and Fourteen:

Gifts from Strange Sources

Why Theists and Atheists
Fight Among Themselves

The Differences That Unite Us

Chapter Twelve
Gifts from Strange Sources

As people with diverse religious viewpoints understand each other better, they can move from hostility to tolerance and from tolerance to respect. Some will even feel appreciation, discovering that people with "false" beliefs may have very helpful insights. As a result, a lifestance that once seemed alien can be a source of unexpected gifts.

In this chapter we will consider the gifts that theists and atheists can give each other, along with one crucial contribution from agnosticism. We will compare two contradictory possibilities: (1) There is a god (meaning a divine person, spirit, or power). (2) There is no such deity. Both perspectives offer benefits that all of us can share, if we approach religious matters with an open and flexible attitude.

Two of the main reasons for having beliefs are that they *fit* and they *work*. Beliefs *fit* in much the same sense that a map of the world resembles the way the world appears – and like that map, there are always distortions. And they *work,* in a broader sense that goes beyond just mapping reality. Beliefs provide important bonuses, including emotional benefits such as comfort, reassurance, and inspiration.

What fits sometimes clashes with what works. A coldly objective description of the world may offer little comfort or inspiration, but some reassuring beliefs ("I'm going to win the lottery") may be hazardous. There is a creative tension between ideas that uplift us and ideas that provide realism and caution.

Let's see how belief in a transcendent god fits and works. Then we'll see how it also fits and works to reject theism.

Theism Fits and Works

Many people, including some atheists and agnostics, find that belief in a divine force or person fits their experience. See if you would answer "yes" to any of the following questions:

❀ Do certain events seem to nudge you in a positive direction, as if someone or something were guiding you?

❀ Does there seem to be a force for good in the world? Do you feel at times that it protects you from harm? When you are in trouble does part of you look to this force for assistance? Do you pray to it, or think in ways that resemble prayer?

❀ When you do things that are helpful or harmful, does it seem as if someone or something knows about it?

❀ Do you sometimes sense an invisible presence, as if a guiding spirit is with you?

Most believers would answer yes to at least some of these questions, and some non-believers would as well. When an atheist or agnostic has one or more of these attitudes, is this a throwback to childhood religion or a flash of spiritual insight? What do you think?

In addition to (sometimes) fitting our experience, faith in a transcendent god also works, and one of the main practical benefits of theism is personification.[209] Because we are persons, we think in personal terms. We want to humanize the universe, imagining that everything is like us.

We do this all the time. The label on Phillips' Milk of Magnesia says this product "works with your body more like nature intended." So does nature have intentions? Is Bayer HealthCare LLC making a corporate pronouncement about the existence of a cosmic mind? Not likely. Nevertheless, I instantly understood that this slogan means the medication works in harmony with the normal functioning of our bodies. We personify often and effortlessly, without even noticing it.

I have mentioned thinking of the world as Mother Earth. Do you ever do that? Obviously Earth is not a female parent, and yet this idea means a lot to many of us. Despite sometimes showing a frightening side, whipping up hurricanes and shaking the ground, Earth generally caresses us in a life-giving embrace. Although I assume that "she" is just a chunk of mindless minerals, I love this orbiting rock-pile, and in a poetic, non-literal way, my Earth-cradle loved me first.

Personal theism allows us to think in relational terms, to feel companioned by the Ultimate. Personification also encourages person-to-person dialogue. As a pastor and psychotherapist I saw parallels between prayerful conversations with God and the gestalt dialogue technique pioneered by psychiatrist Fritz Perls. I noticed that my clients made better decisions using this technique than by just talking about their perplexities in the usual way. Then it dawned on me that this may be what happens in prayer. By praying, we enter into a conversation (whether in reality or in our own imaginations) with hidden sources of inspiration and insight.

> ✎ *Gestalt dialogue.* You can try this technique yourself. Select some minor or medium-sized inner conflict. Imagine you can divide yourself into two people who disagree about how to resolve this issue. Perhaps you have been thinking about switching churches, but part of you fears losing familiarity and good friends. Perhaps you are wondering whether to talk with your son or daughter about religious disagreements. Or perhaps something comes to mind that does not involve religion. Just pick a topic, identify two sides in this controversy, and conduct a conversation, out loud, between the parts of you that favor one side or the other. For instance, the part of you that wants to change churches can talk with the part of you that does not.

The contrast between the two sides will be more clear if you talk out loud, rather than just thinking about the issue. If that's embarrassing or impractical, a written dialogue can also work. Try to continue until you find a resolution. If you're stuck, keep going for at least five minutes more. You may be close to a breakthrough.

Caution: This is a powerful technique! Do not use it for emotionally loaded issues without professional guidance.

The Rev. Garnet McClure suggests that her parishioners compose a letter to God and then write what they see as God's answer. You could also write such a letter to Jesus, Isaiah, Mohammed, the Buddha, Socrates, or an imaginary wise one who knows what you need to hear.

A god who can talk to us is especially helpful when we are struggling with moral dilemmas. Since we are persons, we look to other persons for guidance. We can also look to ethical principles, but such principles may seem like vague abstractions. They lack the motivational mojo of obeying the will of almighty God. It may be easier to obey a person – even an invisible and perhaps nonexistent person – than to be true to an abstract ideal.

Since I am urging an exchange of gifts, let's think about how an atheist (or an agnostic) can use personification without accepting religious doctrines. One could imaginatively personify *love, life, goodness, truth, creativity, humanity, the Earth, the laws of nature, or the entire universe.*

✎ *Poetic personification.* This exercise is meant mainly for non-believers. Theists can use a similar approach, thinking in more traditional terms. Imagine an invisible being who knows what every person should do in order to get the most out of life *and* make the world a better place. Imagine further that this remarkable entity can reveal the ideal way for you to live, and if you follow its counsel you will find happiness and fulfillment. What would this being tell you?

❀ What would it say to do more of? Less of?
❀ What new actions would it suggest?
❀ What surprising and creative ideas would it offer you?

You may want to modify this exercise by making the wise one less godlike. Instead of an invisible being, you could imagine encountering a hyper-intelligent space alien who is friendly to humans and can tell you things that go far beyond what you could discover on your own. What guidance for your life would the extra-terrestrial provide? How do you respond to this "E.T." fantasy, compared to imagining a supernatural entity?

In addition to personification I want to mention two more benefits of theism and show how atheists and agnostics can receive similar payoffs.

First, people want support in dealing with everyday challenges. Many look to God to play this role, and religion gives people such strong emotional support that it may even be good for our health. Dennett has found "growing evidence that many religions have succeeded remarkably well [in] improving both the health and morale of their members . . . ."[210]

Some of my atheist and agnostic parishioners have drawn strength from traditional spiritual disciplines, reinterpreted in secular terms. They practice yoga without becoming Hindus, positive visualization without calling it prayer. Therefore I would respectfully disagree with Christopher Hitchens' claim that "There is no need for us to gather every day, or every seven days, or on any high and auspicious day, to proclaim our rectitude or to grovel and wallow in our unworthiness. We atheists do not require any priests, or any hierarchy above them, to police our doctrine. Sacrifices and ceremonies are abhorrent to us."[211]

I am surprised that Hitchens dismisses the obvious usefulness of regularly focusing on core values, as congregants do during worship. It is so easy to be swept along by life's busy trivialities, so that the merely urgent crowds out the truly significant. And to call ceremonies abhorrent denigrates the remarkable power of ritual. Although Hitchens tries to speak for all atheists in rejecting ceremonies, many unbelievers are moved by weddings, bar and bat mitzvahs, memorial services, or even traditional public worship.

Another benefit is that the idea of god has directional value. It's a pointer, showing us some good places to search for meaning and guidance. It says to look beyond ourselves, beyond who we think we are. Turn away from the repetitious chatter of the mind – listen to a wiser silence. Turn from little worries – look to the broad sweep of life. Turn from preoccupation with our smallness – tap into energy, creativity, wisdom, and love.

Paying attention to higher guidance works, even if we aren't sure where it comes from. If you have a sudden insight or feel profoundly inspired, then you do have the insight and you do feel uplifted, regardless of who or what gave you these gifts. Some say God gives us these blessings. Others say they come from a higher power, a higher self, the voice of reason, or the inner light. I don't much care what we call it, as long as we listen to it.

So theism offers gifts that non-theists can receive in secular terms, reinterpreting traditional religious ideas naturalistically. If you are atheistic or agnostic, *find out what "sings the god-song" for you.* What plays roughly the same positive role in your life that belief in God plays for theists? What do you cherish most deeply? What can you rely upon for healing and transformation? Those who reject the concept of god can look for a related concept, a conceptual cousin of theism. Or if you dislike the very idea of deity, then just add an o to "god" and focus on your vision of the good.

Faithful Translations

An atheist or agnostic can sometimes translate a traditional church doctrine into secular terms, and theists can express secular ideas religiously. Michael Dowd, for example, translates frequently and fluently. After speaking of "partnership with God," he adds, "should you prefer less traditional terminology: *trusting the Universe, trusting Reality, trusting Time.*" "Traditional language declaring 'God is Lord,' and modern expressions like 'Time will tell,' 'Nature bats last,' 'Your ego does not run the show,' and 'All creatures evolve by adapting to their environments,' point to a similar if not identical understanding and experience."[212]

Anthony Freeman translates traditional prayers. One English prayer calls the Queen God's "chosen Servant" who is to be humbly obeyed. For Freeman, "the prayer is an expression of hope for the well-being of our whole country which the Queen, as a figure-head, symbolizes."[213]

As I mentioned above, adding an "o" to god gives us good. If you are a theist talking to an atheist, find out what that person considers supremely good and you can loosely translate that as god. If you are an atheist, find out what a theist considers god, and add another o. One's god-concept is thoroughly intertwined with what one values most. With a little care, we can learn to speak each other's language, albeit with a very thick accent.

Atheism Also Fits and Works

In several ways, then, belief in God fits our experience and works in our lives. It also fits and works to assume that gods do not exist and that we can explain the world in naturalistic terms. Atheism fits the scientific outlook, which we take for granted in many aspects of everyday life. It also fits those periods when God seems to be absent, when the universe seems arbitrary, as if no one is in charge.

Many who love God very much pass through such periods. Even Jesus was said to have cried out on the cross, "My God, my God, why hast thou forsaken me?" (Matthew 27:46) Commenting on God's elusiveness, Tom Owen-Towle suggests that "Yahweh simply likes playing hide-and-seek with us: 'Truly, thou art a God who hidest thyself' (Isaiah 45:15). . . . The metaphorical phrase, 'God hides His face,' occurs over thirty times in the Hebrew Bible. Hence, Yahweh was frequently veiled in the scriptures, even to those who trusted him, so much so that Pascal was moved to assert that no religion that fails to admit the hiddenness of God can be regarded as true."[214]

So in some ways, at some times, atheism may seem to fit the facts better than theism. Furthermore, non-belief works; it offers important gifts both to skeptics and to those who are traditionally religious. Let's consider these gifts by tuning in to Theodore, Althea, and Agnes once last time.

Althea: Atheism is not just saying no to gods. It can also be a positive philosophy with practical benefits. Imagine that your mind is a congress with representatives from various political parties. Some members of this congress belong to the Skeptical Party, the party that says a god probably does not exist. What would we lose if these members were banished from parliament?

Agnes: I'm going to ride along on your coattails and mention some benefits of agnosticism.

Althea: My first idea relates to both atheism and agnosticism. Without skepticism about religion, people might be tempted to treat life on Earth as trivial. Usually belief in God goes hand in hand with belief in an afterlife, so that this present life is only a brief beginning. An old hymn claims that "This world is not my home, I'm just a-passing through."[215]

Agnes: Anthony Freeman does an excellent job of criticizing one-sided other-worldliness, quoting a standard funeral prayer which says "'We give thee hearty thanks, for that it hath pleased thee to deliver this our brother out of the miseries of this sinful world' . . . The whole theme of the service is summed up in one of its sentences: 'Man that is born of woman hath but a short time to live and is full of misery.'"[216]

Theodore: Sounds like the joke about the world's worst restaurant: "The food was absolutely inedible – and the portions were so small!" But come on, folks, you know there are lots of churches and temples that focus on this life. Many Christians emphasize that the kingdom of heaven is at hand, right now. Every moment is precious.

Agnes: Point taken, Theodore. Even so, agnosticism focuses our attention on life here and now, and I think that's good. Maybe our time on earth is a mere eye-blink in an eternity of existence. I hope that is true! But what if it's all we have?

Althea: Here's another benefit of non-belief. Even if atheists are wrong about God, perhaps we can serve as an example of how to find "security amid insecurity." Our non-belief compels us to search for serenity without relying on religion, and many of us do achieve inner peace.

Theodore (smiling): So maybe God is using you for positive purposes after all.

Althea: Why not? Remember the line from Woody Allen's *Stardust Memories?* "To you I'm an atheist. To God I'm the loyal opposition."

Theodore: Of course theists can also find security amid insecurity. We can question our own religious convictions without drowning in anxiety.

Althea: But if I were a theist, I would want to have a sort of fallback position so I could feel positive even if my faith faltered.

Theodore: Say a little more about that.

Althea: People can be religious without completely chaining their own happiness to their belief-systems. They can say, "Yes, I think that God is fully in charge and all will be right with the world. But regardless of whether that is 100% correct, it's still a great blessing to be alive here and now." By including both of these approaches, you get a sort of Plan A – Plan B theology: "Even if some of my beliefs are incorrect, I can still enjoy the miracle of being a living, breathing, knowing, loving human."

Agnes: So a theist might think of atheism (or agnosticism) as a "backup" perspective: "Even if there is no god, I can find beauty and goodness in this Earthly life."

Theodore: Paul Tillich gave us a Plan A - Plan B theology by offering a minimal theism that survives all doubt and skepticism. In this minimalist theology God is the Ground of Being rather than a supreme being who answers prayers by performing miracles. One of his books ends by saying, *"The courage to be is rooted in the God who appears when God has disappeared in the anxiety of doubt."*[217]

Agnes: Although it may be disconcerting to lose some cherished certainty, people often adjust to the change and feel fine later on. Several times I have found myself moving from security to insecurity to a more solid security, and for me this occurs in a way that is predictable and reassuring.

Althea: Christopher Hitchens speaks of this adjustment process, recalling the way he began doubting Marxism, which was for him a sort of secular religion: "Thus, dear reader, if you have come this far and found your own faith undermined – as I hope – I am willing to say that to some extent I know what you are going through. There are days when I miss my old [Marxist] convictions as if they were an amputated limb."[218]

Theodore: What a painful image! By speaking of amputation, he seems to suggest that adjusting to a loss of faith may never be complete.

Agnes: Perhaps, but one reason I can be an agnostic is that I am mostly optimistic about our ability to live without certainty. Regardless of whether we believe or disbelieve, the world is still an exciting and fascinating place. Whether it's religion or brain chemistry that makes us say yes to life, those affirmations can keep on coming. Admittedly, many of us slide into pessimistic habits of thought, and off-kilter hormones push some of us into depression. But in general we show remarkable resilience, bouncing back from all sorts of disappointments.

Althea: Lots of very positive people have an overall outlook that seems disheartening – "there is no guiding intelligence, life has no objective purpose, we live briefly and then vanish forever, and one day the cosmos will grind to a halt, overcome by entropy." I have known many individuals who believe exactly these things and still find contentment. As John Milton wrote, "The mind can make a heaven out of hell or a hell out of heaven." Life is paradise and perdition, all mixed up together. We can hate it or we can love it.

Agnes: I wish I could be sure that goodness is in charge of the universe, that I will live forever, and that everyone will be happy for eternity. In my heart I hope this is all true, but there is no final security.

Theodore: That's why we speak of religious faith more than religious "knowledge." I don't mean rigid or closed-minded faith. But we do have evidence that the creative impetus at the core of reality is powerful and loving. I could be mistaken about this, but if I am, what have I lost? I have lived as if God is with me, always by my side. This helps me keep going when I might otherwise give up. And that is my personal Plan A - Plan B theology. Even if I'm wrong, my beliefs have helped me do what's right and find fulfilment.

ﷺ ﷺ ﷺ ﷺ ﷺ ﷺ ﷺ ﷺ ﷺ ﷺ ﷺ ﷺ ﷺ ﷺ

During these conversations our three friends have sometimes been clumsy or insensitive, but they have been willing to admit their errors and apologize. They have shown respect, empathy, and humility without losing directness and candor. And they have realized that their world-views have limits and potential disadvantages.

Our trio has also exemplified *individual differences.* Although the wide range of individual differences is one of the best-known discoveries of modern psychology, theologians and philosophers still overgeneralize about human nature. They may ignore, for example, the way people vary in their need for religious reassurance. Recall de Chardin's claim that seeing death as the end would "immediately dry up in us the springs from which our efforts are drawn."[219] For many non-believers that is patently untrue.

Plan B

I promised earlier that I would mention one major benefit of agnosticism. By leaving open the question of God, agnosticism can serve as a sort of *universal Plan B*. Part of me can take a leap of faith (or doubt) and live as if there is (or is not) a God, while my agnostic side acknowledges that I could be wrong.

Even those who are traditionally religious may want to create a fall-back position, a simple, Earth-focused philosophy that affirms life's value regardless of whether church teachings are correct. Furthermore, many who believe in God realize that their own theology is just one of many legitimate ways of understanding our world. Like atheists and agnostics, these non-dogmatic theists face the challenge and opportunity of finding serenity without certainty.

Admitting ignorance focuses my mind and heart on what I can know with greater certainty: I am alive. I am bonded in caring with friends and family. I am part of the great human venture, and I want to help make this world a better place. Regardless of whether my personal speculations about great cosmic questions turn out to be correct, if I live by these principles I won't have wasted my days.

The Twelfth Key: Loyalty to a Larger Vision

I want to mention one more unifying idea, a principle that is easily stated but very important:

> ❖ *All of us, theists, atheists, and agnostics alike,*
> *can dedicate our lives to something*
> *greater than ourselves.*

I am convinced that people who identify with larger purposes are "richer" than those who are stuck in self-centeredness – richer in the resonant meanings that turn life into a great adventure. Recall Edwin Burtt's comment that by committing to deeply cherished values we can grow "into a more capacious self which has left its previous boundary behind."[220]

Believers can commit themselves to a larger vision by obeying the will of God, but non-believers can also devote themselves to high ideals. St. Augustine wrote, "Our hearts are restless until we find rest in thee." Compare these words with Parker Palmer's definition of spirituality: "the eternal human longing to be connected to something larger than one's own ego."[221] It feels good to grow toward something larger and lovelier that calls forth the best we can give.

Theists, atheists, and agnostics who sincerely seek a higher vision are kindred spirits despite their differences. *The truly great gap is not between belief and unbelief. It is between those who dedicate their lives to a greater purpose and those who care little for the common good.*

Here is another contrast that seems more important than the gap between theism and atheism. There is a huge difference between those who are rigidly attached to their own opinions and those who realize that other views are also valid. It's like the difference between hearing music through one channel or through surround sound. I admit that for me, the loudspeaker labeled **MY BELIEFS** is much bigger than the others. But sometimes I can faintly hear another strain of music, playing in counterpoint to the melodies I love.

✎ *Gifts from Three Sources.* If you'd like to review the gifts offered by various philosophies and theologies, you can use the radial outline format to list the most important advantages of theism, atheism, and agnosticism. I suggest making a separate outline for each of these options. Or if you want to combine them, try starting off like this:

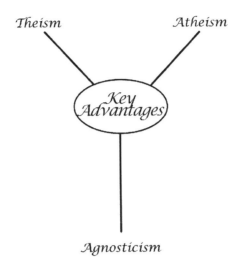

Mark the two most important benefits of each of these perspectives. When your outline is complete, look back and see whether you were surprised by anything you experienced during this exercise.

Summing up: Theists, atheists, and agnostics can receive many gifts from each other if they are willing to approach theology with an open mind and a flexible attitude.

One strength of traditional theism is its emphasis on personification. A god who talks with us is especially helpful when we face moral dilemmas.

Those who reject traditional religion can look for a conceptual cousin of theism, a positive outlook on life that "sings the god-song" in a secular key.

It also fits and works to deny that gods exist. And even if they are wrong about deity, non-believers have pioneered the search for security amid insecurity. Paradoxically, learning to accept absolute insecurity may open the door to inner peace.

Chapter Thirteen
Why Theists and Atheists Fight Among Themselves

Sometimes those who do not believe in God criticize each other, and there are also bitter frictions among theists. In this chapter we will consider ways that theists and atheists can better understand their fellow believers and skeptics.

Varieties of Disbelief

In recent years I have noticed disagreements between what could be called *secular atheists* and *spiritual atheists*. In using these terms I am not suggesting that humanism is neatly divided into sects. Non-believers tend to shape their own ideas in creative and idiosyncratic ways. But speaking very loosely, I call people secular atheists if they find little value in religion, whereas spiritual atheists draw upon resources from the world's faith traditions or invent humanistic versions of religious teachings and practices. Sam Harris, for example, is a spiritual atheist in several respects. There are also secular and spiritual agnostics. Michael Krasny writes that "Though most agnostics eschew organized religion, many . . . take comfort in religious ritual, practice, ceremony, and community."[222]

Let's look at three typical conflict-zones among non-believers.

1. Some atheists and agnostics reject virtually all religious concepts and customs. I have mentioned Christopher Hitchens' abhorrence of religious ceremonies and holidays. But Sam Harris favors invoking the power of ritual "to mark those transitions in every human life that demand profundity – birth, marriage, death – without lying to ourselves about the nature of reality . . . ."[223]

Unbelievers often mix secular and spiritual tendencies. They may despise traditional religion but appreciate yoga, meditation, or Eastern thought, and this opens them to criticism from their fellow skeptics. "At least one atheist Web site displays an amusingly McCarthyite zeal for rooting out religious or spiritual sympathies among supposed nonbelievers."[224]

Atheists and agnostics who are drawn to meditation, personal growth, and/or non-rational experiences *may* be drawn toward traditional spirituality, but each person is unique. Some famous non-believers have valued religion so much that they have even belonged to congregations. Novelist Graham Greene described himself as a "Catholic atheist,"[225] and at one point Kurt Vonnegut "called himself a 'Christ-worshipping agnostic.'"[226]

Many atheists describe the world in semi-religious language. For instance, even though I would mostly characterize Daniel Dennett as a secular atheist, he sometimes sounds like a minister in a liberal congregation. (I mean this as a compliment, of course!) Listen to the way he concludes *Darwin's Dangerous Idea:* "The Tree of Life . . . is surely a being that is greater than anything any of us will ever conceive of in detail worthy of its detail. Is something sacred? Yes, say I with Nietzsche. I could not pray to it, but I can stand in affirmation of its magnificence. The world is sacred."[227]

2. Another source of conflict among non-theists involves speculations that go beyond our current understanding of physical reality. For example, those who try to heal someone's illness by transmitting positive energy are working outside the contemporary scientific paradigm. Sam Harris maintains that there is "data attesting to the reality of psychic phenomena, much of which has been ignored by mainstream science." And lifelong atheist Arthur Koestler left a bequest endowing the chair of parapsychology at the University of Edinburgh.[228]

Harris is also open to something akin to panpsychism, the idea that non-living matter is conscious, and he is interested in reincarnation.[229] Obviously if human beings are born again into new bodies, we are more than just brain processes. Science would need to undergo revolutionary changes to explain how this is so.

Some atheists become upset when non-believers endorse notions such as extrasensory perception. "Do you really buy that hokum?" they may ask incredulously. But even though I am personally dubious about paranormal phenomena, I want to be open to any possibility if there is evidence for it. Harris says that his critics have claimed that *"The End of Faith* is not a truly atheistic book. It is really a stalking horse for Buddhism, New-Age mysticism, or some other form of irrationality."[230] He sees these jibes as narrow-minded, and I agree.

3. Some non-religious individuals accept pre-scientific concepts such as *luck*. Gamblers may believe that they have lucky or unlucky streaks, beyond the obvious fact that games of chance involve random fluctuations. In China, the government has tried for decades to stamp out beliefs which lack scientific confirmation. Yet Beijing has had little success in squelching the pervasive Chinese emphasis on lucky and unlucky numbers, colors, and so on. Even today many Chinese who do not believe in God do believe in luck.

Although well-known atheists such as Dawkins tend to emphasize science, not all skeptics test their personal convictions against research data. I have heard atheists remark that "everything happens for a reason" or "everything happens for the best." Some seem to believe in fate, saying things like, "When your number comes up there's nothing you can do about it." None of these claims could be verified by science or anything else. How could we possibly find out whether *everything* happens for the best? Even so, such untestable notions have widespread appeal. They soothe the sting of tragedy, and (unfortunately) they also help us avoid personal responsibility. My point is that some non-religious people affirm these ideas while others reject them.

It seems odd for non-believers to expect each other to fit into tidy little categories. Freethinkers should be allowed to think freely, and "skeptical orthodoxy" is an oxymoron. If you are an atheist or agnostic, why not give others the latitude that you yourself desire?

Liberal Christians and Biblical Literalists

Many religions are sharply divided into liberal and conservative factions. For the sake of simplicity I will focus on Christianity, but similar controversies roil other religions. As Stanford University chaplain Scotty McLennan reports, "Each group generally dislikes and distrusts the other, which it caricatures, if not demonizes . . . The lines between Christian denominations are barely important anymore by comparison to the lines within each denomination between conservatives and liberals."[231]

Arguments about issues such as abortion, birth control, homosexuality, and women in ministry involve disagreements about how the Bible should be interpreted. A 2007 Gallup poll showed that "About one-third of the American adult population believes the Bible is the actual word of God and is to be taken literally word for word." Literalists accept "inerrancy," meaning that the Bible is free from error. On the other hand, about half of Americans believe that the Bible "is the inspired word of God but that not everything in it should be taken literally."

The Gallup report continues: "Some denominations hold the belief in a literal Bible as a hallmark of their faith. The statement of 'Faith and Mission' of the Southern Baptist Convention, for example, says that: 'The Holy Bible was written by men divinely inspired and is God's revelation of Himself to man. It is a perfect treasure of divine instruction. It has God for its author, salvation for its end, and truth, without any mixture of error, for its matter. Therefore, all Scripture is totally true and trustworthy.'"[232] And Rick Warren's influential book, *The Purpose-Driven Life* contends that "What we need is a perfect standard that will never lead us in the wrong direction. Only God's Word meets that need. Solomon reminds us, *'Every word of God is flawless,'* and Paul explains, *'Everything in the Scriptures is God's word. All of it is useful for teaching and helping people and for correcting them and showing them how to live.'"[233]

If even one verse of either Testament seems to speak for God but does not reflect God's will, this view of Scripture is false. By contrast, the Presbyterian Church's Confession of 1967 states that "The Scriptures, given under the guidance of the Holy Spirit, are nevertheless words of human beings, conditioned by the language, thought forms, and literary fashions of the places and times at which they were written. They reflect views of life, history, and the cosmos which were then current. The church, therefore, has an obligation to approach the Scriptures with literary and historical understanding."

Literalism may seem like "that old-time religion," but it appeared in its modern form long after the birth of Christianity. According to Karen Armstrong the doctrine of inerrancy was first advanced in the 1870s by Hodge and Warfield. Fundamentalists today interpret the Bible "with a literalism that is unparalleled in the history of religion."[234]

This section has been a challenge to write because I strongly oppose literalism. Although I try to hold my own opinions lightly, realizing I could be wrong, some beliefs are clearly false. Aspiring to open-mindedness does not mean anything goes. I see the doctrine of inerrancy as indefensible, and I am astonished that more than a tiny minority accept it. (For massive documentation of inconsistencies within the Bible, some trivial and some quite substantial, see Donald Morgan's list on the Web.)[235] However when I discuss particular Bible passages with those who consider themselves literalists, they are often much more flexible than "literalism" implies. This is one more example of the need to go beyond labels and slogans, to find out what a person actually believes.

Some say that even though humans have made minor errors in writing down God's words, divine intervention protects Scripture from *harmful* mistakes. So here is the key question: Are there important Bible passages which sound as if they were intended to express the will of God, but clearly do not? It is crucial for Christians to talk candidly about such passages. Similar conversations could occur in Jewish and Islamic circles since some Jews and Muslims are literalists, and their sacred books overlap with Christian scriptures.

I will be quoting some verses which undermine literalism, including several which are dangerous or misleading. I will also discuss the way these questionable teachings tie into belief in God. Use these quotes as a springboard for conversation rather than as a club for whacking your literalist relatives. I do not want to provide lighter fluid for starting arguments. And beware of feeling superior to those who treat these strange passages as holy writ. All of us have made mistakes about religion and none can be complacent.

Let me also emphasize that I am not presenting these verses to condemn traditions which draw upon Scripture, e.g., Christianity, Judaism, and Islam. In fact many recoil at these verses precisely because they offend core principles of the Abrahamic religions. Even so, I realize that some who cherish these traditions may feel that their faith is being attacked. Similarly, I might be uncomfortable reading several pages of complaints about Unitarian Universalist writings, even if I happened to agree with every single point!

Problematic Bible Passages

In early Hebrew times, the penalty for doing any work on the sabbath was execution (Exodus 35:2-3). That seems a bit harsh, but they weren't kidding around. In Numbers 15:32-36, for example, God commands Moses to have a man slain for gathering sticks on the Lord's day. Later Jesus was criticized for working on the sabbath (picking grain to eat, and healing the sick). In an earlier time he might have been stoned to death for those actions. His response to his critics was, "The sabbath was made for man, not man for the sabbath" (Mark 2:27).

Notice the startling implication of this teaching. Jesus of Nazareth rejected Biblical literalism! He explicitly contradicted passages in the Hebrew Bible (and the Christian Old Testament). Instead of saying, "Go ahead and stone me to death, as Exodus 35 requires," he placed central emphasis on human well-being. Since Jesus clearly rejected parts of the Bible, anyone who takes his teachings as truth must conclude that inerrancy is in error. Of course, few Jews or Christians today think God wants us to kill those who work on Sunday, even though the Bible orders us to do that.

In Exodus 32 God becomes enraged at his chosen people and decides to punish them severely, but Moses begs him not to "consume" the Israelites. He warns God that the Egyptians will gossip about him. They will say God tricked the Israelites into leaving Egypt so he could kill them in the mountains later on. "And the Lord repented of the evil which he thought to do to his people" (Exodus 32:14). Although some say "repented" is a mistranslation,[236] the most natural reading of the story suggests that Moses did indeed persuade Yahweh to change his mind.

If every verse of the Bible is true, this story "proves" that God does not know the future. If he did, he wouldn't have decided to punish people harshly and then back off. The story also depicts God as ethically fallible, since he came within a whisker of doing something he would later have regretted. I suspect most Christians would prefer to abandon Biblical literalism rather than accept the idea that God's knowledge and goodness are so severely limited.

In the book of Numbers God's prophet Moses supposedly commands genocide and rape: "Now therefore, kill every male among the little ones, and kill every woman who has known man by lying with him. But all the young girls who have not known man by lying with him, keep alive for yourselves" (Numbers 31:17-18). If God gave these brutal orders, this would raise troubling questions about divine morality.

Deuteronomy 20:10-16 offers guidance about conflict resolution: "When you draw near to a city to fight against it, offer terms of peace to it. And if its answer to you is peace and it opens to you, then all the people who are found in it shall do forced labor for you and shall serve you." That's an interesting interpretation of "making peace." If the city does not agree to enslavement, the Israelites are to kill every man. In some similar cases the women and children were also murdered.[237] These savage practices cannot be reconciled with the Hebrew prophetic tradition, nor with teachings of Jesus such as his focus on the value of children. (See, e.g., Mark 10:13-14.)[238]

The next passage prohibits openness to other faiths: "If your brother . . . or your son, or your daughter, or the wife of your bosom, or your friend who is as your own soul, entices you secretly, saying, 'Let us go serve other gods,' . . . you shall not yield to him or listen to him, nor shall your eye pity him, nor shall you spare him, nor shall you conceal him; but you shall kill him; your hand shall be first against him to put him to death, and afterwards the hand of all the people. You shall stone him to death with stones, because he sought to draw you away from the Lord . . . And all of Israel shall hear, and fear, and never again do any such wickedness as this among you" (Deuteronomy 13:6-11). Today if a Christian teenager became Hindu or Muslim and his or her parents murdered their child out of obedience to the Lord, we would think their theology was terribly twisted.

Many Scriptural teachings show a much more highly-developed spirituality. People are moved by the good Samaritan, who saw that a stranger had been robbed and beaten. Even though the victim was from a different ethnic group, the Samaritan expended great effort to make sure he was well cared for (Luke 10:29-37). Imagine someone like the good Samaritan during the Hebrew invasion of Canaan. Suppose while traveling, this compassionate person came upon the smoking ruins of a city that had been leveled by the Hebrews, who thought God had commanded them to kill every creature within its walls. If this Samaritan-like individual stumbled across a survivor, broken and bleeding, what response would we expect? Showing compassion, of course, binding up wounds with loving kindness.

Some of the best-loved Scriptures, such as the Beatitudes of Matthew 5, focus special attention on those who are weak, suffering, and oppressed. Matthew 25:36 says that when God judges us in heaven he will praise some by saying, "I was naked and you clothed me, I was sick and you visited me, I was in prison and you came to me. . . . as you did it to one of the least of these my brethren, you did it to me."

Despite this Biblical concern for those at the bottom of the heap, nineteenth-century preachers proof-texted God's approval of slavery, quoting New Testament passages such as Ephesians 6:5: "Slaves, be obedient to those who are your earthly master, with fear and trembling, in singleness of heart, as to Christ . . . ." Colossians 3:22, First Timothy 6:1, Titus 2:9-10, and I Peter 2:18 echo and elaborate upon this idea. Biblical literalism therefore made it much harder for Christians to oppose slavery. In 1845, for example, the Rev. Richard

Fuller declared, "What God sanctioned in the Old Testament, and permitted in the New, cannot be a sin."[239] In fact, the Old Testament of the Christian Bible doesn't even condemn selling one's own daughter into bondage. Instead, we find rules to regulate this practice (Exodus 21:7-11).

An Internet parody pretends to sincerely ask radio psychotherapist Dr. Laura, "I would like to sell my daughter into slavery, as it suggests in Exodus 21:7. In this day and age, what do you think would be a fair price for her?"

Remembering how the Samaritan treated a man who had been beaten, compare this response to a woman who has been sexually assaulted. "If a man meets a virgin who is not betrothed, and seizes her and lies with her, and they are found, then . . . she shall be his wife, because he has violated her; he may not put her away all his days" (Deuteronomy 22:28-29). No reasonable person today would imagine that God wants a rape victim to marry her rapist. Notice that nothing is said about whether the young woman *wants* to sleep with her assailant every night for the rest of her life.

The cruel customs of that day treated non-virgins as "damaged goods" that no man would want to acquire, so they made her attacker provide for her financially. But they did not understand human experience as we do today. They had never heard of post-traumatic stress reactions, in which victims of some awful experience wake up trembling after reliving it in a dream. If they had known the lasting effects of trauma, they wouldn't have forced her to relive the sexual attack every night when her husband lay down with her. In fact, a loving deity could have commanded the single men of the tribe to treat her as an especially worthy bride. It ennobles us to ease another person's pain, and one way to do that is to show love for someone who has been deeply wounded. If Bible passages are divinely inspired they should give us new wisdom, not just repeat the errors of an ancient culture.

This is only a brief sampling of disturbing verses. For more jaw-droppers, see this endnote.[240]

We could use a bit of lightness after grappling with this grim material, so here's a favorite story of mine about a problematic Bible passage: "A preacher announced that he would preach on Noah and his Ark on the following Sunday and gave the scriptural reference to read ahead of time. A couple of mean boys noticed something interesting about the placement of the story of the Flood. They slipped into the church and glued two pages of the pulpit Bible together. On the next Sunday, the preacher got up to read his text. 'Noah took unto himself a wife,' he began, 'and she was' – he turned the page to continue – 'three hundred cubits long, fifty wide and thirty high.' Then he looked up at his congregation and said, 'I've been reading this old Bible for nigh on to fifty years, but there are some things in it that are hard to believe!'"[241]

People who belong to an Abrahamic faith need to decide whether Scripture is God's *Word* or God's *words*. Those who say that every word of the Bible was dictated by God are forced into all sorts of tortured interpretations, trying to rationalize verses that are obviously harmful if treated as truth. But literalism can be replaced by a values-based interpretation of sacred literature. This would involve reading individual passages in the context of the Bible as a whole, and in the light of moral insights from one's spiritual community. This approach could unify a wide range of believers and help overcome destructive divisions within denominations.

Summing up: Many non-believers reject most or all of the precepts and practices of religion. Others draw upon resources from the world's faith traditions, or invent secular analogues of religious teachings. In addition, some atheists and agnostics embrace parapsychology, panpsychism, reincarnation, luck, fate, and other ideas which contradict the current scientific consensus.

When liberal and conservative Christians disagree, Biblical interpretation is usually a big bone of contention. If Christians face problematic Bible passages squarely and honestly, they may abandon literalism for a more holistic, values-based approach.

Chapter Fourteen
The Differences That Unite Us

Is there a god? And if so, what is this god like? Wrestling with these questions highlights the extent of our ignorance and the value of living with contradictions. Each theological viewpoint can serve as a lookout post, offering the opportunity to observe the world from a particular angle. Those who stand at other posts may discover things which you cannot, and vice versa. So staff your platform faithfully, but don't ignore bulletins from other lookouts.

Putting It All Together

In writing this book, I have tried to combine concepts that are fairly obvious in themselves but which lead to a surprising conclusion: Belief and non-belief can be complementary rather than antagonistic. Even theists and atheists who disagree in very important ways can learn from each other. Let's review the book's main ideas and see how they add up.

The world's most popular "religion" is the worship of our own opinions, the passionate conviction that *"I'm right!"* But whenever large numbers of good-hearted, well-informed, mentally competent individuals persistently disagree about some issue, it is hard to know who (if anyone) is correct.

Psychologists and neuroscientists have discovered that our minds often function irrationally, through mostly-unconscious processes. If we could see an X-ray view of the way we actually construct our convictions, we would probably blush with embarrassment. We might be shocked at the powerful influence of factors such as imitation, ego, social pressure, childhood conditioning, and the urge to conform or rebel.

The conflicting views of theists, atheists, and agnostics may grow out of different basic intuitions. For example, countless believers report that they clearly experience the companionship of God, but non-believers tend to dismiss such testimony. Each opinion seems compellingly true from a certain standpoint. There are no knock-down arguments that prove or disprove deity, no super-duper objective-perspective that shows who is right. As a result, it is absolutely inevitable that good people will disagree about religion.

The difference between belief and disbelief is sometimes merely verbal. For example, some feel that certain aspects of nature are so sacred that they deserve to be called God. Others value the same natural phenomena, but speak of them in secular language. There can even be common ground between atheists and those who believe in a personal deity. If God is beyond our understanding, then when we say that God thinks, feels, makes judgments, acts, and communicates, we are using these familiar human concepts metaphorically, trying to grasp at some shred of truth about the Ultimate. And although many atheists deny that the cosmos has personal characteristics, others maintain that it does manifest key building blocks of personhood, in either a literal or metaphorical sense. One need not believe in God, for example, to think the universe shows evidence of self-organizing intelligence and conscious awareness, or to say that nature responds to our thoughts, emotions, and communications in ways that science does not yet understand.

We are tiny but inquisitive creatures, striving valiantly to comprehend All-That-Is. We grope in the darkness, brushing against mysteries beyond our grasp. We can dress these mysteries in god-language, and then we will be theists. Or we can strip off those holy robes and live as atheists. And so, we place our bets. Yes, there is a deity hidden in the darkness. No, there is not. Or we can stand pat as agnostics. But we cannot float up above it all and say, "Now I see who is right." We need the testimony of both theism and atheism to reflect the full range of human experience. In a very real sense, open-minded theisms and open-minded atheisms are brothers and sisters in disguise.

Ian Markham, a Christian theist, has offered a wonderful insight about our current theological confusion. The diversity of our world-views shows that reality is (for human beings) inherently ambiguous. We say we "believe" in some doctrine precisely because we cannot *know* it is true. "We are all . . . making assumptions that we cannot prove . . . ." Markham concludes that God *wants* us to have multiple orientations. He therefore speaks of "an inevitable provisionality that God has built into the creation." "It is partly because this is the way that God made creation that I am confident God will be merciful to those who opt for a different [i.e., non-Christian] interpretation of the world." "We need to learn to live with divinely intended pluralism . . . ."[242] Well said!

Here is a metaphor of unity-in-diversity: *If life is like a big jigsaw puzzle, each of us is entrusted with a precious handful of puzzle-pieces. Our varied viewpoints add to the whole. They are therefore* **the differences that unite us.**

This is a crucial message of *Bridging the God Gap:* We need many perspectives to unify our world. Theological disagreements will help us find wholeness if we treat other viewpoints as gifts instead of as menacing threats. Our conflicting opinions about deity help to complete us as full human beings. For the most comprehensive picture of ultimate reality we need theists, atheists, agnostics, and others too creative to classify. It may not always be so, but this is where we find ourselves today.

Certainly there are differences between believing or not believing in a God who has personal qualities. But belief and disbelief can gather in love, on the common ground of Mystery. Believers, seekers, and skeptics – all are companions in this astonishing, frightening, thrilling, and exquisitely beautiful adventure of life-as-human.

How to Divide the Pie?

I don't think we should pigeonhole people based on whether they think "God" refers to something real. But if splitting the world into theists and atheists is crude and misleading, what would be a better approach? How should we categorize the truly significant differences among various world-views? I will offer a tentative answer to this question, but I welcome other suggestions. I currently divide theologies into four categories plus some subgroups, realizing that these broad generalizations obscure many complications and exceptions. I will give each group a name and a motto.

❀ 1. *Personal theism, taken literally:* "God is a superhuman person." It is literally correct to say that God thinks, feels, makes judgments, acts, and communicates, in much the same sense that we do except far better. In this country many (but by no means all) literal personal theists are also Biblical literalists.

The next two categories are versions of what could be called *non-literal* or *"broad-brush" theism.* For non-literal theists, God is so astonishingly mysterious that human beliefs about deity are mostly metaphorical. Thus when we say that God is a person, it may be hard to know in what ways this statement is true and in what ways it is false. I call this approach "broad-brush" theism because describing God metaphorically, in terms of our familiar human world, is a bit like drawing an architectural blueprint with a paint-roller – very, very approximate. A more philosophically sophisticated name-tag would be *mysterian* theism. The first subgroup of mysterian theists reveres "my god who helps me," while the second focuses on "our god who helps us." I am not entirely satisfied with my labels for these two categories, but perhaps someone else will invent better ones.

❀ 2. *Relational theism:* "God is my hidden helper." These theists see descriptions of God as metaphorical, but they believe that God provides individual assistance – answering prayers, granting us everlasting life, etc. I use the word "relational" to emphasize that on this view, God relates to us as individual persons.

❀ 3. *Impartial theism:* "God is our hidden helper." These theists worship a deity that does not single out specific individuals for special treatment. It supports us in a more general way, as the sun generally supports life by shining all over the Earth.

The practical differences between options 2 and 3 are enormous. It matters a lot to a father whether God might cure his daughter's terminal illness. It matters to all of us whether death ends personal consciousness. And note that many believers straddle the line between 2 and 3. If talk about God is metaphorical, it may not be clear whether our hidden helper intervenes on behalf of particular persons.[243]

It's another big step from broad-brush theisms to the final category:

❋ 4. *Physicalism*: "Everything is made of matter." There is no supernatural kingdom beyond the scope of science. Some physicalists respond with awe, gratitude, or even reverence to the amazing material universe, while others do not.

Most physicalists are atheists or agnostics, but quite a few, including some of my Unitarian Universalist parishioners, could be called *theistic physicalists*. They revere some aspect of the material cosmos, something so precious they consider it sacred, such as love, creativity, human goodness, the highest values, or the universe as a whole. Those who define God as love, for example, are theistic physicalists if they think love resides only in physical beings such as humans.

In this theological typology, which groups of theists and atheists seem closely akin to each other? How could they discover this, in dialogue? As examples, here are three fictional conversations. In the first dialogue, an atheist addresses a theistic physicalist:

Atheist: When you tell me that God is a symbol of the highest values you can know, do these "values" exist outside of the material world?

Theistic physicalist: Values don't float around in an Esoteric Realm of Venerable Abstractions. Our values are part of us, and we are physical creatures. I am a naturalistic theist because I find these values worthy of worship.

Atheist: I detest the word "worship," but I want to translate your ideas into terms that make sense to me. Instead of, "I worship values," how about, "The highest values are worthy of our total commitment"?

Theistic physicalist: Exactly. Evidently you and I see eye to eye about what really matters.

ða ða ða ða ða ða ða ða ða ða ða ða ða ða

Impartial theist: You say there is no persuasive evidence that God exists, but I disagree. I believe something greater than we are created the universe. Even so, I don't think this difference should divide us.

Agnostic: That's encouraging, but why not?

Impartial theist: I know very well that I could be wrong. Theology is mostly speculative. And even if I'm right, I do not see God as waving a magic wand to establish world peace or to get me a job if I pray hard enough. Also, I have no idea what happens after death. On that issue, I'm as agnostic as you are.

Agnostic: Then welcome to the club. For most practical purposes, we're on the same team.

ða ða ða ða ða ða ða ða ða ða ða ða ða ða

The theist in the previous dialogue doesn't see God as helping individuals. The next dialogue includes someone who does:

Relational theist: You and I have been assuming that we have almost opposite opinions about God.

Atheist: You believe God is a person, answers prayers, and resurrects us after we die.

Relational theist: And you deny all of that. But after thinking it over, I realize that I am not especially attached to these opinions. I think I'm right, of course, and my beliefs give me comfort. But if I'm wrong, and death is the end, so be it.

Atheist: To meet you halfway, I should magnanimously declare that I have absolutely no emotional attachment to my own rejection of religion. But it's not nice to lie to a friend, and frankly, I think theology is bunk. Nevertheless, I can grudgingly admit that every one of us is guessing about all this. If I end up standing at the pearly gates, I hope St. Peter will say, "Your beliefs were WAY off base, but we know you were doing your best. We'll give you an A for effort and let you in."

Relational theist: So I'll see you in Heaven – if I'm right about religion, and if God looks kindly on your skeptical old soul.

ⁿ⸾ ⁿ⸾ ⁿ⸾ ⁿ⸾ ⁿ⸾ ⁿ⸾ ⁿ⸾ ⁿ⸾ ⁿ⸾ ⁿ⸾ ⁿ⸾ ⁿ⸾ ⁿ⸾ ⁿ⸾

For those who like charts, here is a rough schematic showing potential overlap among various lifestances. "Yes" means there is often considerable common ground between two world-views. "No" means common ground is rare or nonexistent. For example, I think there is seldom much conceptual common ground between an atheist and a literal personal theist, so I typed No in the box located in the last column of the top row. My assessments are subjective, and you may wish to copy this grid and fill it in as you choose. Items in [brackets] duplicate earlier boxes, but are included to make the chart easier to read.

	Personal Theism (Literal)	Relational Theism	Impartial Theism	Theistic Physicalism	Atheistic Physicalism
Personal Theism (Literal)		**Yes**[244]	**No**	**No**	**No**
Relational Theism	[Yes]		**Yes**[245]	**No?**[246]	**No?**
Impartial Theism	[No]	[Yes]		**Yes**[247]	**Yes**
Theistic Physicalism	[No]	[No?]	[Yes]		**Yes**
Atheistic Physicalism	[No]	[No?]	[Yes]	[Yes]	

This chart highlights important comparisons and contrasts. For instance, most theists who are sure God answers individual prayers do have strong substantive disagreements with atheists, but those who think of God as a broadly benign entity or energy could see some atheists and agnostics as their philosophical allies. We need to reconsider the way we classify philosophies of life, revealing key similarities and differences without being confused by theological labels.

Self-Assessment

Think about your overall reaction to the material explored in this book. Which ideas have been especially appealing? And why? Which ones have you resisted, and why?

When have you found yourself pushing away an idea that might be correct, but would rub against your preconceptions? What experiential and behavioral signals have alerted you that you are feeling "threatened with expansion?" Are you beginning to notice these signals in the midst of daily life?

Out of all the ideas we have considered, what are the *three* that you most want to focus upon in the future?

The Introduction to *Bridging the God Gap* included a radial outline of your beliefs about God. I invite you to try a similar exercise now (before looking back at your earlier draft).

If you are a theist, write "God" in the center of a blank sheet of paper. Think of the most important aspects of your current ideas about deity, and list these in a circle, all around the page.

If you are an atheist or agnostic, you could follow the same instructions. Or you could write "Ultimate Reality" in the center instead of "God." Then list core attributes of reality, including your understanding of the physical world, the larger universe, and whatever may lie beyond the cosmos.

What was it like this time to sketch your outline? Has your concept of God shifted? If so, then regardless of whether your theology has become more traditional or less so, give yourself credit for being open to change.

Beyond Simple Agnosticism

In preparing this book I have generally tried to set aside my own beliefs. I have wanted to function as a fair-minded conceptual facilitator, helping readers clarify their own ideas and appreciate the ideas of others. Perfect objectivity is obviously unattainable, but if we aim for the stars we're more likely to hit the rooftop. Now as we complete our journey together as writer and reader, I will close with some non-objective personal comments.

I have come to realize that my view of the world is rather odd, in at least two important ways. First, after reflecting on the limits of human knowledge since college days, I have made modest progress in realizing that my views may be mistaken. I still pay regular visits to the Great Shrine of Schriner-is-Right, but I am less and less comfortable falling down in adoration before my own opinions. I also feel increasingly out of step with those who assume that their beliefs are clearly correct.

My second peculiar attitude is that I think we have barely begun our voyage of discovery. This puts me out of sync with those who picture themselves as living near the end of human inquiry rather than the beginning. I see *Homo sapiens* as the tadpole instead of the frog, the acorn instead of the full-grown oak. After all, the scientific method has been extensively practiced for only a few hundred years. I expect discoveries to pile up even faster now, with computers mining data at an ever-quickening pace. We ain't seen nothin' yet.

My future-focused perspective makes a big difference in the way I think about all sorts of things, including political, religious, and scientific matters. For example, I think theoretical physics is still in its infancy. Do you recall the discussion in Chapter Eight about how the laws of the universe appear to have been precisely designed for human existence? While it is intriguing to speculate about this issue, it seems remarkably optimistic to imagine that we know much about it today.

Since we can see where we've been but not where we're going, it's easy to treat the distant future as if it will not be. Such "chronological nearsightedness" can trick us into thinking we have learned about as much as we're going to. It's like driving a car while looking only in the rear view mirror.

Because great truths are still unfolding, I see the future of both science and religion as vastly open. If there are mysterious spirits, energies, or powers, I think researchers will someday detect them, perhaps in a thousand years, perhaps in a million. Unless some duplicitous deity (or demon) is deliberately trying to trick us, we will probably bump into him/her/it/them. But will our exploration of deeper and deeper layers of reality actually disclose a supreme being? I would be delighted if we came across something that literally resembles a caring and compassionate super-person, someone wise and good who communicates with us and works for our welfare. We desperately need such an ally, but I am not counting on this outcome.

My emphasis on ignorance may sound like agnosticism, and my willingness to accept paradox resembles post-modernism.[248] Post-modernists tend to reject overarching accounts of how-it-all-is, such as the Christian story of fall and redemption or the current scientific model of the cosmos. Some post-modernists yearn for new forms of theism, less dogmatic and perhaps more poetic than standard church doctrine. John D. Caputo mentions "what Mark C. Taylor calls 'a/theology,' something situated on the slash between theism and atheism, in a space of undecidability before things are definitively settled one way or the other . . . ."[249]

Besides challenging traditional theism and atheism, these considerations also undercut the sort of agnosticism which only asks whether Christian theology is right about God. Such a narrow focus leads to odd logic, such as the claim that since the Christian God either does or does not exist, we can start by assuming that the chances are 50-50 and then see which way the evidence moves us.

This would be like a simple card game, turning over a playing card after betting on red or black, but this is no two-card wager. Visualize instead a Las Vegas style "shoe" holding six decks or more – and some of these decks contain cards we have never seen before. Instead of the King of Diamonds we may be dealt the Count of Rubies and have no idea how to play it. The theological possibilities before us are vast and unknowable.

This is not your grandfather's agnosticism.

Although broad-spectrum agnosticism has merit, such a wide-ranging skepticism might tempt us to throw down our cards in frustration. "It's all so confusing. I'll just forget about religious issues." Or: "I'll just believe what suits my fancy, since one opinion is as good as another."

How can we combine radical openness with a personal philosophy that is both realistic and inspirational? I find it helpful to imagine myself moving between two locations, and I invite you to consider the following metaphor:

Imagine that we are explorers in an enormous wilderness, the seemingly endless forest of How-It-All-Is. We have pitched our tents in a base camp which we share with those of other faiths and philosophies. Our base camp is constructed out of *shared knowledge, consensus wisdom, common values, and common projects.* These commonalities give us a starting point, but each of us spends most of our time tramping off along some personal pathway that calls to us with special appeal. This personal path is mapped according to our chosen wager about ultimate reality. Some adventurers head off in a theistic direction. Others chart the terrain of secular humanism. We take the risk of belief or unbelief, and see where that journey takes us. From time to time we can return to our common encampment, to swap stories with other explorers and replenish our supplies.

In my own explorations I focus on values which seem worthy of worship (in the old sense of "worthship," reverence for what is of lasting worth). I hold myself accountable to these values. When I stray from them I know I have fallen short of standards that are absolutely precious to me. Such values include the search for truth, intellectual humility, continuous self-correction, respect for those who see things differently, nurturing close relationships, helping those in need, caring for one's body, working for the common good, living as if humanity has a future, and commitment to the interdependent web of existence. Since I treat these principles as sacred I could qualify as a naturalistic theist, but I am cautious in using god-language to refer to aspects of the natural world, and I dislike limiting myself with theological labels.

I am glad to have had a little success in becoming open-minded. Using the analogy of binocular vision, my dominant eye now sees the world in terms of the physical facts of science and the human meanings that move my heart. The other eye sees a swirl of additional possibilities. The first eye seems to see clearly – but does it see accurately? The second eye observes a blurry kaleidoscope, but parts of this pastiche are exquisitely lovely.

That is how life seems from my lookout post. How does it seem from yours?

How to Keep Narrowing the Great God Gap

This book has encouraged open-mindedness, respectful communication, empathetic understanding, and humility about our own opinions. It takes work to develop these virtues, and here are some suggestions about how to keep doing that.

One way to follow up is to choose two or three exercises from the book, and practice them. See the List of Exercises, right after this page.

We can also become more open-minded by reading what the "opposition" has to say. Browse "For Further Reading," immediately after the List of Exercises.

✎ *Journaling and blogging.* If the themes of *Bridging the God Gap* are important to you, consider keeping a journal or a weblog of your reflections and experiences. Make notes about conversations with people whose philosophies of life contrast with your own, and about books and articles on religion. You could include poems, drawings, and even songs about religious and philosophical topics. You could also comment on the way you experience the exercises listed in this book.

If you are interested in offering programs based upon *Bridging the God Gap,* you will find information about obtaining a leader's guide on p. 209.

You can also follow through by reading the endnotes. Not wanting to overwhelm readers with quotes and technical details, I have included many stimulating quotations and important clarifications in these notes.

List of Exercises

Here are the 21 exercises and structured practices which were highlighted with text boxes and marked with this icon: ✎

Introduction:

1. *Radial Outline: God.* Write the word "God" in the center of a blank sheet of paper. Think of different aspects of your opinions about God. Arrange these in a circle around the page, linking them to the central topic with solid lines like spokes of a wheel. You might include comments about whether God exists, what God is like, what has led you to believe or disbelieve, arguments in favor of your position, advantages and disadvantages of believing as you do, as well as doubts and confusions. One spoke might represent past beliefs. (For examples of radial outlines, see pp. 7-8.)

Chapter Two:

2. *Open-Mindedness Exercise.* Think of some philosophy of life that you consider false, and ask yourself questions such as these:

Am I smarter than *everyone* who believes it?

Am I morally superior to *all* of its adherents?

Do I think I know certain facts that *every one of them* has overlooked?

If you could not answer yes to these questions, is there any good reason for being absolutely certain that you are correct? *(And remember that I am also challenging readers who disagree with you about theology: What makes them assume that you are deluded?)*

3. *Mind-Closing Cues.* Develop the habit of noticing how you feel when you encounter something that challenges your viewpoint.

What do you experience when your mind is "threatened with expansion"? What warning signals occur when you are blocking out a good idea that might disturb preconceptions? If you can identify cues that alert you when this is happening, you can learn to catch your own mind-gate just as it starts to swing shut.

Some cues are felt in the body and others are more "mental." Perhaps you will sense a mild irritation or a sudden desire to focus on something else. Do you tighten your jaw? Do you repeat your own arguments more emphatically, either silently or out loud? Do you feel like backing away or turning away?

4. *Bias Inventory.* Try listing at least five of your own biases about religious issues. What are you emotionally inclined to believe, so that it would be hard to make a factual case that convinced you otherwise?

5. *The Split-Level Strategy.* Think of some way in which you feel ambivalent about whether there is a god or what that god is like. Try reflecting on one side of this ambivalence today and the other tomorrow. Do this a few times till you begin to develop an intuitive sense about when to switch perspectives. With practice you can sense two opposite inclinations at almost the same instant.

Chapter Three:

6. *The Positive Pause.* We have all noticed the difference between automatically reacting and reacting after reflection. *The first response is habit. The second response is yours.* One fine time to practice the positive pause is in ticklish talks about religion. When you start to react automatically to some comment about theology, take a couple of deep breaths while you think of a more carefully-considered response.

7. *Inconsistency List.* Identify at least five of your own philosophical inconsistencies about questions such as the following. What is God like? What is our highest purpose? Is there life after death?

Are paranormal phenomena such as predicting the future fact or fiction?

Chapter Four:

8. *Role Reversal.* Do a little play-acting with a friend and imagine yourselves trading viewpoints about religion. You may want to talk about what it would feel like to believe as your friend believes, say what could lead a person to accept this lifestance, and identify what you see as the greatest strength of this position.

9. *Restate, Then Reply.* Suppose Alice and Bob are talking and Alice speaks first. Bob will then restate the gist of Alice's message, and Alice will say whether Bob got it right. *Bob cannot reply to Alice's message until he restates it to Alice's satisfaction.* Then when Bob replies, Alice summarizes his message till her restatement meets with Bob's approval, and so on. Try this for some agreed-upon period of time, perhaps 20 minutes.

10. *Look Back and Learn More.* Try mentally replaying a conversation to see what you can learn. Think of ways that you and your friend were positive and helpful. Then recall ways that you were less than constructive. Give yourself credit for candidly assessing your own mistakes. If you pray, pray for guidance about areas of difficulty. If you do not pray, focus your mind on your commitment to speak and listen in useful ways.

Chapter Five:

11. *Similarity List.* Think of a person who disagrees with you about religion and list at least 25 ways you are similar. If you get stuck, write down trivialities: "We both love lemon meringue pie." Then keep writing. Look back at your list and see how your feelings have changed.

12. *That's Me.* When you are around someone who disagrees with you about God, pay attention to this individual and *imagine that he or she is you.* Does he look tired? You can picture yourself

with the same weary expression. Is she drinking tea? Imagine you are the one lifting the cup to your lips. See how your feelings change as a result.

13. *The Light and the Wound.* Think of someone you love. Close your eyes and imagine him or her radiating bright light. What personal qualities shine through in that glow? Then remember that this person is in some way wounded. All of us bear scars. Can you sense where it hurts?

Now think of someone whose religious convictions clash with your own. Hold that person in your thoughts long enough to sense and appreciate his or her light. Then focus on this person's woundedness. How do your feelings change?

14. *Radial Outline: Our Common Humanity.* Make a radial outline with "Human Kinship" in the center. List ideas about our common humanity in a circle around the page. Which of these seem most important to you? Which commonalities help you feel close to others?

Chapter Six:

15. *Your Higher Power.* Think of an aspect of your life where you seem to need some assistance, where despite your best efforts you have been unable to make much progress. Now think of something that could help you, something or someone you can turn to when the chips are down. Look for opportunities to find support, encouragement, insight, and inspiration from this source of strength.

Chapter Eight:

16. *Peak Experiences.* Recall some of your own "peak experiences," special states of mind that gave you a fresh outlook on life. What seemed to call forth these extraordinary states of awareness? What aspects of these episodes would you like to keep fresh and alive? How could you encourage similar breakthroughs in the future? If you are traditionally religious, can you imagine construing

these experiences in non-religious terms? If you are an atheist or agnostic, can you imagine someone else being in a similar frame of mind and considering it religiously significant?

17. *Pro and Con: Is There a God?* By using the radial outline format or by making a list, write down what you see as the strongest arguments for and against the existence of God. Start by deciding which sort of deity you will be considering, such as the God of the Christian Bible. List arguments for God's actuality on one side and arguments against on the other.

Chapter Twelve:

18. *Gestalt Dialogue.* Select some minor or medium-sized inner conflict. Imagine you can divide yourself into two people who disagree about how to resolve this issue. Conduct a conversation, out loud, between the parts of you that favor one side or the other.

The contrast between the two sides will be more clear if you talk out loud, rather than just thinking about the issue. If that's embarrassing or impractical, a written dialogue can also work well. Try to continue until you find a resolution.

Caution: This is a powerful technique! Do not use it for emotionally loaded issues without professional guidance.

19. *Poetic Personification.* This exercise is meant mainly for non-believers, but theists can use a similar approach, thinking in more traditional terms. Imagine an invisible being who knows what every person should do in order to get the most out of life *and* make the world a better place. Imagine that this remarkable entity can reveal the ideal way for you to live, and if you follow its counsel you will find happiness and fulfillment. What would this being tell you? What would it say to do more of? Less of? What new actions would it suggest? What surprising and creative ideas would it offer you?

Alternatively, you could imagine encountering an intelligent space alien who can tell you things that go far beyond what you could discover on your own. What guidance for your life would the extra-terrestrial provide? How do you respond to this "E.T." fantasy, compared to imagining a supernatural entity?

20. *Gifts from Three Sources.* Use the radial outline format to list the most important advantages of theism, atheism, and agnosticism.

How to Keep Narrowing the Great God Gap:

21. *Journaling and Blogging.* Keep a journal or a weblog about religion. For a list of possible themes, see the text box on p. 195.

For Further Reading

Karen Armstrong, *A History of God,* New York: Gramercy Books: 1993.

Karen Armstrong, *The Case for God*, New York: Knopf, 2009.

James P. Carse, *The Religious Case Against Belief*, New York: Penguin Books, 2008.

John B. Cobb, Jr., *The Process Perspective II: Frequently Asked Questions about Process Theology* (edited by Jeanyne B. Slettom), St. Louis, Missouri: Chalice Press, 2011.

Don Cupitt, *Above Us Only Sky: The Religion of Ordinary Life,* Santa Rosa, California: Polebridge Press, 2008.

Richard Dawkins, *The God Delusion*, New York: Houghton Mifflin, 2006.

Daniel C. Dennett, *Breaking the Spell*, New York: Penguin Books, 2006.

Michael Dowd, *Thank God for Evolution,* New York: Plume, 2009.

Greg Epstein, *Good Without God*, New York: HarperCollins, 2009.

Anthony Freeman, *God in Us*, Thorverton, United Kingdom: Imprint Academic, 2001.

Sam Harris, *The End of Faith*, New York: W. W. Norton & Company, 2005.

John F. Haught, *God and the New Atheism*, London: Westminster John Knox Press, 2008.

Christopher Hitchens, *God Is Not Great*, New York: Twelve (Warner Books), 2007.

Bruce E. Hunsberger and Bob Altemeyer, *Atheists: A Groundbreaking Study of America's Nonbelievers*, Amherst, New York: Prometheus Books, 2006.

Mark Johnston, *Saving God: Religion after Idolatry*, Princeton, New Jersey: Princeton University Press, 2009.

Michael Krasny, *Spiritual Envy*, Novato, California: New World Library, 2010.

Ian S. Markham, *Against Atheism: Why Dawkins, Hitchens, and Harris Are Fundamentally Wrong*, Chichester, United Kingdom: Wiley-Blackwell, 2010.

Michael Martin, ed., *The Cambridge Companion to Atheism*, New York: Cambridge University Press, 2007.

Scotty McLennan, *Jesus Was a Liberal*, New York: Macmillan, 2009.

Bradley Monton, *Seeking God in Science: An Atheist Defends Intelligent Design*, Ontario, Canada: Broadview Press, 2009.

William R. Murry, *Reason and Reverence*, Boston: Skinner House Books, 2007.

Tom Owen-Towle, *Wrestling With God*, San Diego: Barking Rocks Press, 2002.

Eric Reitan, *Is God a Delusion?* Chichester, United Kingdom: Wiley-Blackwell, 2009.

Rabbi Steven Carr Reuben, *A Nonjudgmental Guide to Interfaith Marriage: Making Interfaith Marriage Work,* USA: Xlibris, 2002.

Douglas Stone, Bruce Patton, and Sheila Heen, *Difficult Conversations: How To Discuss What Matters Most,* New York: Penguin Books, 2000.

Charles Taliaferro, *Dialogues about God*, Lanham, Maryland: Rowman & Littlefield, 2009.

Kevin J. Vanhoozer, ed., *The Cambridge Companion to Postmodern Theology,* New York: Cambridge University Press, 2003.

Definitions

Theological terms are used in many different ways. I favor the following definitions, but I do not claim that mine is the only legitimate usage or even the best. Note that I typically capitalize God when the word refers to a specific entity, while using lower case for generic uses of the term.

I call people *agnostics* if they are sincerely ambivalent about whether any sort of deity exists. Some agnostics say the question of God's existence is inherently unanswerable, while others say that it may be answerable in the future.

I call people *atheists* if they confidently reject traditional ideas of deity and they do not affirm any other god-concept.

Deism means belief in a god who created the universe and its laws, and then allowed it to run on its own. Most deists would deny that God speaks to us as individuals or responds to our prayers.

Lifestance is a relatively new term for a person's overall orientation toward how-it-all-is. Some lifestances are theistic and some are not.

Monotheism is the belief that there is only one god, in contrast to *polytheism*, the belief that there is more than one.

Naturalistic theism views God as an aspect of the natural world rather than as a supernatural entity. Some naturalistic theists revere something within nature as we currently understand it, something so precious they consider it sacred. Others believe in a godlike power that is part of the cosmos but which science cannot currently detect.

Pantheism is the belief that everything is God, whereas *pan-entheism* is the belief that God permeates everything. By analogy, water can permeate a sponge without being identical to the sponge.

Some pan-entheists say that the universe is within God, but that God is also more than the universe.

Personal god: a god who does things people do, such as thinking, feeling, making judgments, acting, and communicating. In this book, *personal theism* means belief in such a god. Because Christians often speak of Jesus as their *personal savior,* the term "personal god" may sound like the god which one personally worships. That would be a different use of this term.

Theism: As noted in Chapter One, I use words such as *"theist, theism, and theistic"* broadly, in referring to any viewpoint which affirms that God is a reality. If someone says God is real instead of imaginary or fictional, I will call that person a theist. This understanding of theism includes both naturalistic and supernaturalistic theism, as well as monotheism, polytheism, deism, pantheism, and pan-entheism.

World-view: See "lifestance," above.

I have also coined several terms which I hope will help us identify meaningful differences among theological positions. See the section of Chapter Fourteen called "How to Divide the Pie?"

About the Author

Dr. Roger "Chris" Schriner is Minister Emeritus of Mission Peak Unitarian Universalist Congregation in Fremont, California. He graduated from the University of Redlands, majoring in religion, philosophy, and psychology. He received a Doctorate in Religion from Claremont School of Theology and an M.S. in Marriage, Family and Child Counseling from the University of LaVerne. His honors thesis at Redlands examined the ethical thought of theologian Paul Tillich. His dissertation at Claremont dealt with nuclear weapons policy.

In addition to ministry, Dr. Schriner worked for 20 years as a psychotherapist, and he has led personal growth workshops throughout his career. *Bridging the God Gap* is his fifth book. His previous publications include *Feel Better Now* and *Do Think Twice: Provocative Reflections on Age-Old Questions.*

Dr. Schriner has also studied comparative religion, neuroscience, philosophy of mind, and various spiritual disciplines. He lives in Fremont, California with his wife Jo Ann.

Workshop Leader's Guide

By August, 2011, *Bridging the God Gap: A Guide for Workshop Leaders* will become available. This resource will include outlines of one-session and three-session programs, plus other formats. It will retail for under $10 including shipping. Contact revschriner@aol.com or revschriner@gmail.com. If these addresses are no longer operative, search online for the author's blog or website.

ENDNOTES

Because this book was written for the general public, the endnotes do not use standard academic notation. For example, I have not used Latin abbreviations, except for *ibid.* when two successive endnotes quote the same source.

Most of the endnotes that contain text are complete in themselves, so that readers need not refer to citations in earlier notes or flip back through the book to find the endnote's context.

To reduce the number of endnotes I have not provided sources for brief quotations which are easily accessed on the Internet.

1 "Atheism," second definition, *Webster's New International Dictionary, Second Edition, Unabridged,* p. 173. Similarly, the authoritative *Oxford English Dictionary, Second Edition, Volume One* defines an atheist as "one who practically denies the existence of a God by disregard of moral obligation to him; a godless man" (p. 745).

2 Penny Edgell, Joseph Gerteis, and Douglas Hartmann, *American Sociological Review,* April, 2006, p. 212, http://www1.umn.edu /news/news-releases/2006/UR_RELEASE_MIG_2816.html. Those who emphatically reject theism are often called "avowed" or "militant" atheists. Compare "avowed homosexual" and "militant Marxist." People use such language in referring to stigmatized individuals.

3 http://www1.umn.edu/news/news-releases/2006/UR_RELEASE _MIG_2816.html. The denigration of atheists is so common that people hardly notice it. For example, Jack Huberman reports that "At the 2002 opening of the United States Congress, a Rabbi Latham mentioned 'the evil doctrine of atheism.' Not one member of Congress protested the bigoted remark."
Did you just do a double-take at the suggestion that it's bigoted to insult atheism? What if the rabbi had referred to "the evil doctrine

of Presbyterianism?" Huberman also stated that "In 1996, NBC's Tom Brokaw introduced a jokey segment" dealing with Madalyn Murray O'Hair, "who had been missing for a year, by saying: 'She had the dubious distinction of being known as America's most outspoken atheist.' As FAIR (Fairness and Accuracy In Reporting) noted: 'It's impossible to imagine Brokaw making light of the disappearance of someone who has the "dubious distinction" of being a leader of America's Catholics or Jews'" (http://www. huffingtonpost.com/jack-huberman/how-to-save-our -secular-a_b_40523.html).

4 Penny Edgell, Joseph Gerteis, and Douglas Hartmann, *American Sociological Review*, April, 2006, p. 215. Note also that the authors of a study of North American atheists were "astonished" that so many had paid a heavy price for disbelief. "Even in the San Francisco area – arguably the most tolerant part of the United States – [about half] reported that being a nonbeliever had produced difficulty with relatives and friends. The figure was predictably higher (67 percent) and the price often far greater in Alabama and Idaho" (Bruce E. Hunsberger and Bob Altemeyer, *Atheists: A Groundbreaking Study of America's Nonbelievers,* p. 55). As one atheist commented, ". . . I keep quiet about it. People assume you're heartless, shallow, amoral, and it calls their own beliefs into question. Atheism *greatly* disturbs people" (p. 47).

5 A comment by Henry Stone illustrates the difficulty of talking openly about non-belief: "I am an atheist. It's hard to say this without sounding either boastful or apologetic, and I don't mean to be either." Cited by Tom Owen-Towle, *Wrestling With God*, p. 148. Owen-Towle's book includes numerous illuminating quotations about deity.

6 Richard Dawkins, *The God Delusion*, p. 324.

7 According to Charles Taliaferro, theism is often defined as "the belief in an all-powerful, all-knowing, all-good, necessarily existing Creator of the cosmos" (*Dialogues about God*, p. 6). By this definition many who passionately believe in God could not qualify as theists. For one thing they might never have even considered

whether God *necessarily* exists, in the technical, scholarly sense of "necessarily." And although many scholars insist that theism must refer to a personal being, those who say that God is everything are called pan*theists* even if they think of God as non-personal. Similarly, naturalistic theists do not typically think of God as a personal entity, and yet they too are called theists. To cut through all of this confusion, I simply refer to those who affirm God's reality as theists, regardless of whether their deity is personal or impersonal.

8 Monotheism, of course, is the belief that there is only one god, while polytheism is the belief that there is more than one. This is partly a matter of what labels we decide to use. Some religions define subordinate beings as lesser gods, while others, such as Christianity, refer to them as angels. Pantheism is the belief that everything is God, whereas pan-entheism is the belief that God permeates everything. By analogy, water can permeate a sponge without being identical to the sponge. Sometimes pan-entheism is "defined as the view that the world is within God, though God is also more than the world" (Philip Clayton, *The Cambridge Companion to Postmodern Theology*, ed. Kevin J. Vanhoozer, p. 206).

9 Notice that there is a double standard in many people's understanding of theism and atheism. Often those who think God does not exist but are not quite sure are classified as agnostics, whereas those who think God does exist but are not quite sure are categorized as theists. While it is considered normal for believers to have theological doubts, it is commonly assumed that atheists are absolutely adamant in rejecting theism.

10 http://humanisteducation.com/class.html?module_id=1&page=2.

11 John F. Haught, *God and the New Atheism*, p. 44.

12 Karen Armstrong, *A History of God,* p. 354.

13 See John F. Haught, *God and the New Atheism*, p. 93. In *The Case for God*, p. 323, Karen Armstrong calls the correspondence between atheist philosopher J. J. C. Smart and theist J. J. Haldane, "a model of courtesy, intellectual acumen, and integrity . . . ."

14 Tim LaHaye, cited by William R. Murry, *Reason and Reverence*,

p. xix. In a similar vein Jerry Falwell proclaimed, "We're fighting against humanism, we're fighting against liberalism . . . we are fighting against all the systems of Satan that are destroying our nation today . . ." (http://www.hillmanweb.com/reason/pious_quotes .html).

15 http://www.infidels.org/library/modern/mathew/arguments.html reports George H. W. Bush's comment about non-believers, and adds the following: "After Bush's election, American Atheists wrote to Bush asking him to retract his statement. On February 21st 1989, C. Boyden Gray, Counsel to the President, replied on White House stationery that Bush substantively stood by his original statement, and wrote: 'As you are aware, the President is a religious man who neither supports atheism nor believes that atheism should be unnecessarily encouraged or supported by the government.'"

16 Penny Edgell, Joseph Gerteis, and Douglas Hartmann, *American Sociological Review*, April, 2006, p. 229. Bush made similar comments while being interviewed by *Christianity Today* on May 26, 2004: "There's nothing more powerful than this country saying you can worship any way you want, or not worship at all." Although accepting those who don't worship may not be the same as accepting those who don't believe, these statements seem to show a general respect for the non-religious. See http://www.christianity today.com/ct/2004/121/51.0.html.

17 *Ibid., p.* 230, italics added.

18 *The Argus,* January 6, 2010, p. A14.

19 http://pewforum.org/docs/?DocID=490.

20 Daniel C. Dennett, *Breaking the Spell*, p. 253. Although he is an atheist, he engaged in extended conversations with believers in preparing to write *Breaking the Spell: Religion as a Natural Phenomenon.*

21 Christopher Hitchens, *God Is Not Great*, p. 45.

22 James Wood, *The New Yorker,* August, 2009, p. 76. Michael Krasny, who has interviewed prominent atheists on the radio, feels

that they sometimes come across as "cocksure" (*Spiritual Envy,* p. 27).

23 John F. Haught, *God and the New Atheism*, pp. 93, 68.

24 James P. Carse, *The Religious Case Against Belief*, pp. 2, 31.

25 Karen Armstrong, *The Case for God*, p. 304. Italics are in the original text. For her critique of the new atheism see pp. 301-09.

26 Philosopher Mark Johnston scoffs at Dawkins and his allies, referring to them as "undergraduate atheists." In *Saving God*, p. 39, he writes, "The 'undergraduate' atheists, if we may call them that without reflecting adversely on actual undergraduates, uncritically share a defective premise with their secret fundamentalist allies, namely, that religion is essentially supernaturalist . . . (Did they meet in a back room with the fundamentalists, long ago, to agree to collaborate in the task of obscuring real religion?)" Thus Johnston seems to agree with Karen Armstrong that only atheists and fundamentalists see God as a supernatural entity, in spite of overwhelming statistical evidence that this is a mainstream doctrine.

27 Karen Armstrong, *The Case for God*, p. 308.

28 http://pewforum.org/news/display.php?NewsID=19716. This data on belief in miracles was reported in early 2010.

29 http://people-press.org/reports/pdf/287.pdf. Most of those who believe Jesus is coming again are unsure when this will occur, but 20% expect it within their own lifetimes.

30 Tom Krattenmaker, *USA Today,* August 23, 2010, p. 9A.

31 Rodney Stark, cited by Daniel C. Dennett, *Breaking the Spell*, p. 191.

32 Scotty McLennan, *Jesus Was a Liberal*, pp. 45, 60.

33 See Mark Johnston, *Saving God,* and John B. Cobb, Jr. *The Process Perspective* and *The Process Perspective II: Frequently Asked Questions about Process Theology* (both edited by Jeanyne B. Slettom).

34 Tom Owen-Towle, *Wrestling With God*, p. 13.

35 Ian S. Markham's book is called *Against Atheism*. He does a good job of critiquing non-belief without insulting non-believers.

36 William R. Murry's *Reason and Reverence* supports a non-theistic version of religious humanism.

37 http://www.webster.edu/~woolflm/martineau.html.

38 Pamphlet, "The Garrison-Martineau Project."

39 Eric Reitan, *Is God a Delusion?* p. 8.

40 James P. Carse, who directed New York University's Religious Studies Program for thirty years, shows that religion can awaken our sense of the mysterious rather than closing people's minds with pat answers. In *The Religious Case Against Belief*, he writes that spiritual seekers "may begin to acquire the art of seeing the unknown everywhere, especially at the heart of our most emphatic certainties" (p. 3).

41 Corey J. Hodges, *The Salt Lake Tribune,* June 27, 2009, p. C4. This survey was conducted by the Pew Forum on Religion and Public Life.

42 "In a recent article in the secularist journal *Philo* Quentin Smith laments what he calls 'the desecularization of academia that evolved in philosophy departments since the late 1960s.' 'Naturalists passively watched as realist versions of theism . . . began to sweep through the philosophical community, until today perhaps one-quarter or one-third of philosophy professors are theists, with most being orthodox Christians. . . . [I]n philosophy, it became, almost overnight, "academically respectable" to argue for theism, making philosophy a favored field of entry for the most intelligent and talented theists entering academia today'" (William Lane Craig, in *The Cambridge Companion to Atheism,* ed. Michael Martin, p. 69). Stephen Law cites somewhat different statistics, claiming that "about 15 percent of philosophy professors and philosophy graduate students are theists" (*Free Inquiry,* February/March, 2011, p. 7).

43 Jesus of Nazareth, Matthew 7:3. Unless otherwise noted, all quotations from the Christian Bible are from the Revised Standard Version.

44 Ibn al-Arabi (1165-1240), quoted by Karen Armstrong, *A History of God,* p. 239. Italics added.

45 Steven Carr Reuben, *A Nonjudgmental Guide to Interfaith Marriage,* p. 31.

46 Charles Taliaferro, *Dialogues about God,* p. xii.

47 Here are some of my biases about spiritual matters:

1. If an idea about spirituality is new and creative, it's better than old and ordinary ideas.

2. The future of religion is more important than its past.

3. Biblical literalism leads to inconsistent thinking and dangerous behavior.

4. Claims of paranormal phenomena, such as extrasensory perception, are almost always false.

5. Finally, I am often dubious about doctrines that perfectly fulfill deep human desires, such as the desire to live forever. *These doctrines may be true anyway,* but it's hard for us to tell because we want so much to believe them.

Some of these biases are probably correct, in general. Nevertheless, my intense commitment to such principles can keep me from seeing important exceptions. In thinking about which items on this list are the most questionable, I would select #1 and #4.

48 "We don't know what the universe is made of (most of it seems to be 'dark matter,' but we don't know what dark matter is)" (Bradley Monton, *Seeking God in Science: An Atheist Defends Intelligent Design,* p. 116).

49 James P. Carse, *The Religious Case Against Belief,* pp. 3-4, 16-17.

50 George Lakoff, *Moral Politics,* pp. 14-15.

51 Bruce Bode, *Quest,* May, 1993, p. 4.

52 Bruce Bode, cited by Tom Owen-Towle, *Wrestling With God,* pp. 22-23.

53 Chris Schriner, *Do Think Twice: Provocative Reflections on Age-Old Questions,* Chapter Eleven and Appendix.

54 Some would say the brain manifests neural activities which are *correlated with* thoughts and beliefs, rather than being *identical to* thoughts and beliefs. In any case, our thoughts and beliefs do seem to be altered by changes in the brain.

55 To learn more about practical implications of neuroscience I suggest two books by psychologist Robert Ornstein – *Mindreal* and his older classic, *The Evolution of Consciousness*. Ornstein provides many examples of the way our beliefs are generated by unconscious factors.

56 Robert Ornstein, *The Evolution of Consciousness*, p. 2.

57 Benedict Carey, *New York Times,* June 21, 2005, p. F1.

58 Frances West, cited by Tom Owen-Towle, *Wrestling With God,* p. 17.

59 David Duncan, *DiscoverMagazine.com*, May, 2009, pp. 68, 70.

60 Most of my current internal contradictions involve issues of meaning and value. For example, I value individualism, maximizing personal freedom, and yet I know that exaggerated individualism has hurt our society. This creates a dissonance which I have yet to re-solve.

Another ethical issue involves how much to enjoy one's own pleasures and how much to sacrifice for others. And I am not sure how to balance the value of human well-being versus the well-being of other animals. I think I should be a vegetarian, but I am not.

I also have mixed feelings about our human future. *Homo sapiens* is marvelously inventive and resilient, but the challenges of population, resource depletion, terrorism, nuclear proliferation, and environmental degradation are daunting.

I have puzzled about the enigma of conscious experience for 20 years. I think I now understand how consciousness could occur within the brain, but at times the mystery seems as impenetrable as ever.

Later we will discuss moral relativism. In *Do Think Twice,* I offer solutions to the problems posed by relativism, but I wonder if I have glossed over some vexing questions about this issue.

61 Some research data "suggest that children are predisposed to assume both design and intention behind natural events, prompting some psychologists and anthropologists to believe that children, left entirely to their own devices, would invent some conception of God" (Matthew Iredale, *the philosophers' magazine*, first quarter, 2010, p. 51).

62 Phil Zuckerman, in *The Cambridge Companion to Atheism,* ed. Michael Martin, p. 61. For a critique of the claim that our brains are programmed for theism, see Daniel C. Dennett, *Breaking the Spell,* pp. 138-41.

63 M. D. Faber, *The Psychological Roots of Religious Belief,* p. 20. Does Faber's analysis show that belief is irrational? A theist might respond by saying, "God has created us for communion with deity, and our brains are designed to make this possible. Childhood dependency prepares us for accepting our ultimate and absolute dependency on the Ground of Being, and this is entirely appropriate."

64 For helpful communication tips and techniques read *Difficult Conversations: How To Discuss What Matters Most,* by Douglas Stone, Bruce Patton, and Sheila Heen.

65 http://www.sweetreason.org/past.htm.

66 Steven Carr Reuben, *A Nonjudgmental Guide to Interfaith Marriage,* p. 35.

67 *Ibid.,* p. 38.

68 *Ibid.,* p. 39.

69 Michael Dowd, *Thank God for Evolution,* p. 128.

70 Steven Carr Reuben, *A Nonjudgmental Guide to Interfaith Marriage,* p. 68.

71 *Ibid.,* p. 66.

72 *Ibid.,* p. 52. Here's the rest of Rabbi Reuben's list:

7. If it were up to me, our involvement with my religion . . .
8. If I had the nerve, I would tell my boy/girlfriend . . .
9. When I think about Jesus, I feel . . .
10. If I never had anything to do with religion again . . .

73 *Ibid.*, p. 18.

74 *Ibid.*, p. 208.

75 *Ibid.*, p. 204.

76 Paul Tillich, *Love, Power, and Justice,* p. 25.

77 David Spangler, *Blessing*, p. 4.

78 Carl Sagan, cited by William R. Murry, *Reason and Reverence,* p. 114.

79 http://www.bereavedparentsntx.org/Newsletter/2002/October20 02/October02.htm. From *We Bereaved,* by Helen Keller.

80 http://quote.robertgenn.com/auth_search.php?authid=148.

81 Rudolf Otto, *The Idea of the Holy,* pp. 25-40, 68-70.

82 Karen Armstrong, *A History of God*, p. 391.

83 *Random Acts of Kindness*, Conari Press, p. 70.

84 *The Quran,* cited by John B. Noss, *Man's Religions,* p. 739.

85 Greg Epstein, *Good Without God*, p. 171.

86 Aldous Huxley, cited by Tom Owen-Towle, *Spiritual Fitness,* p. 343.

87 Tony Larsen, sermon, "Theology of the Mensch." Quotation confirmed in personal correspondence.

88 *The Cambridge Dictionary of Philosophy,* ed. Robert Audi, p. 188. Some writers contrast theism and deism, but I use "theism" in a broad sense to cover all god-concepts that treat deity as real.

89 *The Oxford Companion to Philosophy,* ed. Ted Honderich, p. 182.

90 William R. Murry, *Reason and Reverence*, p. xvi.

91 Differences among naturalistic theists can be subtle. For example, theists who revere some aspect of nature may worship this aspect *as it is currently understood by science*, or with additional features that go beyond science. Thus cosmic creativity could be viewed as the purely physical unfolding of the universe after the Big Bang, or as that plus some sort of "creative impulse" which has not yet been discovered by researchers.

92 Videotape, "The Garrison-Martineau Project."

93 William R. Murry, *Reason and Reverence*, pp. 8-9, xvii.

94 Richard Dawkins, *The God Delusion*, pp. 12-13.

95 Part Thirteen of a YouTube video series showing a debate about God between Dinesh D'Souza and Daniel Dennett.

96 See http://www.gallup-international.com/survey15.htm. These results came from the International Millennium Survey which studied religious attitudes in sixty countries. The same survey showed that worldwide, only 45 percent thought of God as a person, and 30 percent thought of God as "some sort of spirit or life force." (Twenty-five percent did not fall into either category.) Apparently those who believe in a personal god are actually in the minority. However it would be helpful to know in more detail what people typically meant by "spirit or life force."

97 Anthony Freeman, *God in Us: A Case for Christian Humanism*, p. 21.

98 *Ibid.*, pp. 8, 18.

99 *Ibid.*, p. 19.

100 Don Cupitt, *Taking Leave of God,* p. 166. See also Cupitt's recent work, *Above Us Only Sky.*

101 Alexie Crane, cited by Tom Owen-Towle, *Wrestling With God*, p. 29. Crane has stated in personal correspondence that he is also comfortable describing himself as a pantheist.

102 Alcoholics Anonymous World Services, Inc., *Alcoholics Anonymous*, p. 12.

103 Alcoholics Anonymous World Services, Inc., *Came to Believe,* pp. 100, 114-15, and 85.

104 James Wood, *The New Yorker,* August, 2009, p. 76.

105 Karen Armstrong, *The Case for God*, p. ix. Jewish spiritual teachers may have been more consistent in recognizing that statements about deity tend to be metaphorical. According to Karen Armstrong, Judaism does not enforce theological orthodoxy: "Any official doctrine would limit the essential mystery of God" (p. 74). And in Islam, "the Koran is highly suspicious of theological speculation, dismissing it as *zanna*, self-indulgent guesswork about things that nobody can possibly know or prove" (p. 143).

106 In some cases it may be impossible to say whether something is definitely a person. Does a chimpanzee have enough of the building blocks of personhood to qualify? What about a gifted young chimp that is raised by humans in an enriched environment that stimulates thinking, creativity, and close relationships with people and other chimps? Or what about an advanced computer in the year 10,000? Might its internal processes qualify as thoughts, feelings, perceptions, beliefs, and desires? What about intelligent machines in the year 10,000,000? "Person" is a vague and abstract idea, very difficult to pin down precisely.

107 http://washingtontimes.com/news/2006/nov/12/20061112-125119-7426r/.

108 *Ibid.*

109 A person could deny that God has a male body while maintaining that God's mind or personality is male, but this claim falls apart if we consider it closely. Much of "male" consciousness is due to having male anatomy, just as female consciousness is partially shaped by dealing with the possibility of pregnancy. And personality traits that are considered male are only true statistically (if at all). In general, men are more prone to violence, but a particular man may be less violent than a particular woman. In addition, many aspects of maleness are socially constructed, but this would not be true of a supreme being. God wasn't raised by doting parents who handed

"him" a blue blanket and little fire trucks, while giving pink dollies to his celestial sister. Once we subtract out all of these factors, does even a trace of masculinity remain?

110 Roy Phillips, personal communication.

111 Karen Armstrong, *The Case for God*, p. 310.

112 Richard Dawkins, *The God Delusion*, p. 11.

113 Albert Einstein, cited by Karen Armstrong, *The Case for God,* p. 268.

114 Albert Einstein, cited by Michael Dowd, *Thank God for Evolution,* p. 117.

115 Albert Einstein, cited by Christopher Hitchens, *God Is Not Great*, p. 271. Einstein is still being quoted out of context by those who believe God is a supernatural being. For example, Rick Warren used Einstein's famous statement that "God doesn't play dice" to support the idea that God carefully plans each of our lives (*The Purpose-Driven Life,* p. 22). This is as blatant a distortion of Einstein's intent as if an anti-gambling organization had used this quote to show that Albert wanted to ban crap games.

116 Albert Einstein, cited by Scotty McLennan, *Jesus Was a Liberal*, p. 51.

117 http://atheism.about.com/library/quotes/bl_q_TEdis.htm.

118 Michael Dowd, *Thank God for Evolution*, p. 46.

119 http://messianic.nazirene.org/science_proves.htm.

120 http://pewforum.org/docs/?DocID=490.

121 Henry Stone, cited by Tom Owen-Towle, *Wrestling With God*, p. 148.

122 Anthony Freeman, *God in Us: A Case for Christian Humanism*, p. 42.

123 Ric Masten, *Ric Masten Speaking,* p. 1.

124 http://www.youtube.com/watch?v=iw7J15TeDG4&feature=Pla-

yList, from Part Six of the Dennett - D'Souza debate about God.

125 Brian Wren, "Bring Many Names," *Singing the Living Tradition,* #23.

126 Michael Dowd, *Thank God for Evolution*, p. 129.

127 Nick Cardell, *First Days Record,* January 1993, p. 9.

128 For discussions of proofs of the existence of God, read Richard Dawkins, *The God Delusion*, Chapter Three; Karen Armstrong, *The Case for God*, pp. 142-46; Daniel C. Dennett, *Breaking the Spell*, pp. 240 ff.; and Eric Reitan, *Is God a Delusion?* Chapters Five and Six.

129 If you like the dialogue approach, I recommend *Dialogues about God*, by Charles Taliaferro. His entire book consists of a series of conversations representing various positions, including theism and atheism.

130 For Part One of the debate between Daniel Dennett and Dinesh D'Souza, see: http://www.youtube.com/watch?v=iw7J15TeDG4&f eature =PlayList.

131 For evidence from physics see Bradley Monton, *Seeking God in Science: An Atheist Defends Intelligent Design*, especially pp. 76 ff.

132 Daniel Dennett mentioned the possibility of other universes besides our own in Part Seven of the debate between him and Dinesh D'Souza: http://www.youtube.com/watch?v=SryFVhNfvow &feature=related.

133 Philosopher Bradley Monton, an atheist, has written a book which evaluates intelligent-design arguments, including the claim that physical laws were fine-tuned for our benefit. "Ultimately," he concludes, "I don't think very much evidence is there, but that conclusion can only be reached after careful evaluation of the arguments . . ." (*Seeking God in Science: An Atheist Defends Intelligent Design*, p. 7). Perhaps the book should have been subtitled *"An Atheist Studies and Rejects Intelligent Design,"* but that's a bit cumbersome. In any case, Monton is unusually fair-minded in assessing the data. Importantly, he notes that fine-tuning

arguments "are the sorts of claims about which even competent physicists disagree. For example, Nobel prize winning physicist Steven Weinberg has said that he is 'not impressed with these supposed instances of fine-tuning.' . . . I've read a lot of the literature on the fine-tuning argument, but I've never seen an opinion poll of experts, so it's not clear to me what the majority do believe regarding the fine-tuning evidence. However, it is clear to me that the promulgators of the fine-tuning argument aren't relying on such an opinion poll" (p. 81).

134 In the YouTube video of a debate between philosopher Daniel Dennett and theologian Alvin Plantinga, Plantinga asks, "And how much support does the argument from design actually offer theistic belief anyway? Perhaps it suggests belief in the existence of a very powerful and knowledgeable being or group of beings, but that's a very long way from theism." See http://www.youtube.com/watch?v=bz3Tovcyn2g&p=372AF60FD2600C88&playnext=1&index=1. And "cosmologist Edward Harrison has suggested that perhaps the universe was created by intelligent beings living in another universe" (Ian S. Markham, *Against Atheism: Why Dawkins, Hitchens, and Harris Are Fundamentally Wrong*, p. 14).

135 Stephen Hawking has said that "The quantum theory of gravity has opened up a new possibility, in which there would be . . . no edge of space-time at which one would have to appeal to God or some new law . . . The universe would be completely self-contained and not affected by anything outside itself. . . . It would just BE" (http://atheism.about.com/library/quotes/bl_q_SHawking.htm).

136 Phil Zukerman in *The Cambridge Companion to Atheism,* ed. Michael Martin, p. 109.

137 On p. 86 of *Is God a Delusion?* Eric Reitan discusses the mixed results of research into the power of prayer.

138 Daniel C. Dennett, *Breaking the Spell*, p. 275.

139 http://www.christianitytoday.com/ch/131christians/denominationalfounders/wesley.html.

140 Acts 9:1-9; 22:6-16; 26:12-17.

141 Richard Dawkins, *The God Delusion,* p. 88.

142 According to a 2009 study by the Pew Forum, about half of all Americans say they have had a "moment of sudden religious insight or awakening." Certainly many of these moments have seemed like contacts with God. "This is . . . much higher than in surveys conducted in 1976 and 1994 and more than twice as high as a 1962 Gallup survey (22%). . . ." Furthermore, "Among self-described atheists, agnostics and the 'secular unaffiliated' (i.e., those who describe their religion as 'nothing in particular' and say that religion is not important in their lives), [18%] say they have had a religious or mystical experience" (http://pewforum.org/docs/?DocID=490).

143 Eric Reitan, *Is God a Delusion?* p. 141.

144 Daniel C. Dennett, *Breaking the Spell*, p. 250.

145 Marni Harmony, cited by Tom Owen-Towle, *Wrestling With God*, p. 142. I added the first set of ellipses.

146 Don Cupitt, who sees God as a symbol rather than as a real entity, suggests that "In general, mystical experience is very common, very diverse, and occurs in every religion and in people of no religion. It is interpretatively highly ambiguous. It certainly does not specially lend itself to a theistic interpretation: on the contrary, so far as there is any consensus or general drift in the testimony it is probably towards monism rather than theism" (*Taking Leave of God,* p. 31).

147 Anthony Freeman, *God in Us: A Case for Christian Humanism*, p. 17.

148 Karen Armstrong, *The Case for God*, p. xvi. The eminent theologian Paul Tillich also denied God's existence. Instead, God is the Ground of Being, the ground of all that exists. It could be that Tillich thought of deity as a deeper and more mysterious sort of reality than anything else we know. Perhaps God, while not existing as we understand existence, is *more real* than things such as rocks and people. Thus Mark Johnston maintains that Tillich's Ground of Being has been misinterpreted "as fabulously abstract rather than

the most concrete aspect of things . . ." (*Saving God*, p. 98). On the other hand, Tillich did sometimes use "God" and "Ground of Being" as labels for something rather abstract, such as "depth." "If you can say in complete seriousness that life itself is shallow, then you are an atheist; but otherwise you are not. They who know about depth know about God" (cited by Tom Owen-Towle, *Wrestling With God*, p. 32). By suggesting that anyone who experiences life as rich and meaningful is in touch with the Ultimate, Tillich baptized many atheists as honorary believers.

149 http://www.albertmohler.com/2009/09/14/a-tale-of-two-atheists/.

150 *Ibid*.

151 James Wood, *The New Yorker,* August, 2009, p.78. Sigmund Freud said something similar in *The Future of an Illusion*: "Philosophers stretch the meaning of words until they retain scarcely anything of their original sense. They give the name of 'God' to some vague abstraction which they have created for themselves; having done so they can pose before all the world as deists, as believers in God, and they can even boast that they have recognized a higher, purer concept of God, notwithstanding that their God is now nothing more than an insubstantial shadow and no longer the mighty personality of religious doctrines." http://www. adolphus.nl/xcrpts/xcfreudill.html.

152 Karen Armstrong, *The Case for God*, p. ix. Armstrong provides extensive evidence for the claim that Christianity, Judaism, and Islam have often maintained a respectful silence about what God is like. On p. 126 she mentions an approach to theological reflection in which one first affirms what God is, including God's existence; then denies those affirmations, saying for example that God does not exist; and then *denies the denials*. This conceptual discipline is intended to disintegrate our use of typical words and concepts in speaking of the Ultimate.

153 Armstrong definitely rejects some common teachings about deity, such as the idea that God created plants and animals. Life originated because of natural selection, Armstrong says, and not because of divine planning. See Karen Armstrong, "Man vs. God,"

http://online.wsj.com/article/SB1000142405297020344010457440
05030643556324.html.

154 Charles Taliaferro, *Dialogues about God*, p. 19.

155 http://en.wikiquote.org/wiki/Bill_Watterson.

156 Some religious leaders who have fervently denied that God can
be described merely meant that our descriptions (although helpful)
are inadequate. Ross Douthat observes that even though early Christian writers were "reticent" in discussing the divine nature, they
made very specific claims about God's actions. Augustine, for
example, believed that Jesus literally rose from the dead. See *The
New York Times,* October 1, 2009, http://www.nytimes.com/2009/10
/04/books/review/Douthat-t.html.

157 Richard Dawkins, *River Out of Eden,* p. 133.

158 *Ibid.*, pp. 96, xii.

159 Eric Reitan, *Is God a Delusion?* pp. 49 and 195.

160 David Bumbaugh, "Toward a Humanist Vocabulary of
Reverence," Boulder International Humanist Institute, February 22,
2003, http://archive.uua.org/news/2003/vocabulary/bumbaugh.html.

161 The Rev. Tom Owen-Towle's listing of categories of unbelief
includes "cheerful atheists" who "live confidently and comfortably
atheos – *without* but not *against* the notion of deity. They harbor no
belief rather than disbelief. They are more accurately termed
nontheists than atheists. In any case, these seekers are essentially at
peace, both spiritually and socially, living void of metaphysical
reference" (Tom Owen-Towle, *Wrestling With God*, p. 30).

162 During the Inquisition, suspected heretics were tortured until
they either confessed or succumbed. Confession was an extremely
attractive option, because those who admitted heresy were often
executed quickly rather than being slowly roasted to death. (See Sam
Harris, *The End Of Faith,* pp. 80-92.) Similar techniques were used
during various panics about witchcraft, when Christian leaders took
Exodus 22:18 literally: "You shall not permit a sorceress to live"
(Karen Armstrong, *A History of God,* p. 275).

163 Sam Harris, *The End of Faith*, pp. 13, 45.

164 David Wulff, cited by William R. Murry, *Reason and Reverence*, p. 118.

165 "For example, a group of scholars . . . at the U.S. Institute of Peace concluded that 'One must see contemporary religious violence as an expression of tendencies always present in the religious life of humanity'" (Scotty McLennan, *Jesus Was a Liberal,* p. 116).

166 In *The Case for God*, p. 191, Karen Armstrong notes that the Thirty Years' War killed about one-third of the people of central Europe.

167 Daniel C. Dennett, *Breaking the Spell*, p. 55. Jack Huberman, editor of *The Quotable Atheist*, also notes that religion "ensures at least a weekly reminder . . . of the Larger Scheme of Things" (p. xii).

168 Alison Gopnik, *The Philosophical Baby,* p. 218.

169 "Robin Gill's excellent study on *Churchgoing and Christian Ethics* does demonstrate that ultimately religious people do behave better than their non-churchgoing counterparts" (Ian S. Markham, *Against Atheism: Why Dawkins, Hitchens, and Harris Are Fundamentally Wrong*, p. 127). However one anonymous reviewer offers a different assessment: "Drawing chiefly on data from the U.K., Gill contends that churchgoing Christians are not that different from their fellow citizens..." (http://www.leaderu.com/ftissues/ft0002/reviews/briefly.html).

170 Sam Harris, *The End of Faith*, p. 65.

171 Richard Dawkins, *The God Delusion*, p. 308.

172 Daniel Dennett suggests that religions sometimes hide behind three "veils." First, they teach doctrines that are virtually impossible to disprove, such as claims about what heaven is like. Next, they say that certain special doctrines are mysteries beyond comprehension. And finally, they forbid people to ask questions about these mysteries. (See *Breaking the Spell*, pp. 163-65.)

173 Martin Luther, cited by Richard Dawkins, *The God Delusion*, p. 190.

174 Martin Luther, First Psalm Lectures, *Luther's Works,* Vol. 11, p. 285, http://jmm.aaa.net.au/articles/14223.htm. Luther also wrote, "Faith must trample underfoot all reason, sense, and understanding, and . . . know nothing but the word of God" (http://www.hillman web.com/reason/pious_quotes.html).

175 http://www.brainyquote.com/quotes/authors/w/william_jennin gs_bryan.html. A sentimentalized version of the idea that faith trumps reason shows up in the Christmas movie, *Miracle on 34th Street:* "Faith is believing in things when common sense tells you not to." This line appears twice in the film.

176 John F. Haught, *God and the New Atheism*, pp. 5, 13.

177 Holmes Rolston III, cited by John F. Haught, *Ibid.,* p. 46.

178 Part Thirteen of a debate about God between Dinesh D'Souza and Daniel Dennett, http://www.youtube.com/watch?v=ADLjLcS2 kJs&feature=related.

179 *The Economist*, July 11, 2009, pp. 59-60. *Christianity Today* called this Papal encyclical "a brief against secular materialism . . ." (http://www.christianitytoday.com/ct/article_print.html?id=84058).

180 Rick Warren, *The Purpose-Driven Life,* p. 38.

181 Daniel C. Dennett, *Breaking the Spell*, pp. 279-80.

182 Benjamin Beit-Hallahmi, *The Cambridge Companion to Atheism,* ed. Michael Martin, p. 306. And according to Bernard Spilka, Ralph Hood, and Richard Gorsuch, "Most studies show that conventional religion is not an effective force for moral behavior or against criminal activity" (http://www.humanismbyjoe.com/religion _nontheism_unethical_behavior.htm).

183 William R. Murry, *Reason and Reverence*, p. 121.

184 Alison Gopnik, *The Philosophical Baby,* pp. 211-12.

185 Recent research suggests that humans are born with the tendency to care about others and help them in time of need. "Human infants as young as 14 to 18 months of age help others

attain their goals, for example, by helping them to fetch out-of-reach objects . . . They do this irrespective of any reward from adults (indeed external rewards undermine the tendency) . . ." (Felix Warneken and Michael Tomasello, "The roots of human altruism," *British Journal of Psychology*, August 2009, p. 455). In one study, these tykes had to "surmount an array of obstacles to pick up the object for the other. This can be quite effortful for toddlers who have just started to walk. But even these obstacles did not hinder them from helping the other person . . . ." They also helped "even when they had the alternative to play an attractive game" (p. 460). And "infants as young as 12 months of age begin to comfort victims of distress" (p. 458). By contrast, Rick Warren asserts – without a bit of evidence – that "Babies by nature are completely selfish. They think only of themselves and their own needs. They are incapable of giving; they can only receive" (*The Purpose-Driven Life*, p. 182). This fits well with the theological doctrine of innate human depravity, but it does not fit well with the facts.

186 Greg Epstein, *Good Without God*, p. xi.

187 Michael Krasny, *Spiritual Envy*, p. 64.

188 Plato, cited by Alex Byrne, *Boston Review*, March/April 2007. See http://bostonreview.net/BR32.2/byrne.php.

189 Gottfried Wilhelm Leibniz, *Discourse on Metaphysics*, p. 1.

190 Don Cupitt notes that "the Buddha put spirituality above theology by exalting the Dharma above the Gods. The Way comes first. Get the Way right, and talk of the Gods can be allowed to make its own kind of sense as best it can" (*Taking Leave of God*, p. 8).

191 One difficult task for moral relativism is how to evaluate people like Adolf Hitler. Were Hitler's actions truly horrible, or did he just have unusual standards of good and evil? In another book I have maintained that "if Hitler had been thinking clearly, he would have seen that *he was evil according to his own moral code*. He was a diabolical monster by his very own standards, but he was confused about that." For my rationale see *Do Think Twice: Provocative Reflections on Age-Old Questions*, p. 111.

192 Rick Gore, "Extinctions," *National Geographic,* June, 1989, p. 670. "Extinctions have claimed 99 percent of all species that have ever lived" (p. 669).

193 Will Cloughley, personal correspondence. A Zen koan is a sort of riddle, presented by a Zen master to a disciple. The koan cannot be solved through "rational" ways of thinking.

194 http://www.religion-online.org/showarticle.asp?title=3350. See also Michael Dowd's interview with John B. Cobb, Jr., December 9, 2010: http://evolutionarychristianity.com/blog/audio-downloads/.

195 I will generally use terms such as "immortality," "afterlife," "life after death," and "eternal life" as synonyms, even though these are not precisely identical.

196 TV journalists who have used the atheists-in-foxholes cliché "include Katie Couric, Bill Weir, Tom Brokaw, and Bob Schieffer. [Weir] later retracted his statement." After receiving letters from atheists, Bob Schieffer "issued a public apology" (http://www.dbs keptic.com/2008/11/23/a-skeptical-analysis-of-there-are-no-atheis ts-in-foxholes/).

197 Arthur Schopenhauer, http://www.bps.lk/olib/wh/wh144-p.html.

198 http://www.kqed.org/epArchive/R909241000. Armstrong made these comments on September 9, 2009 in a radio interview with Michael Krasny. Her view is that only Christianity and Islam have made the afterlife central, and even there it is often seen as something like a parable rather than a definite statement of fact.

199 Anthony Freeman, *God in Us: A Case for Christian Humanism,* p. 45.

200 Teilhard de Chardin, cited by Eric Reitan, *Is God a Delusion?* p. 215.

201 During a memorial service on June 24, 1980, Robert Ormes shared this quotation from Helen Worthington Gauss, a descendant of the great mathematician Carl Friedrich Gauss. Ormes reported that she described herself as an atheist. Verified by Robert's son Jonathan, personal communication.

202 See http://www.crystalclarity.com/kriyananda/chap_33.html#76. Theologian Paul Tillich believed in eternal life, but he did not think of this as a continuation of consciousness after death. He even wrote that "Endless living in finitude would be hell," and by this he evidently meant living on as an individual person. And in *What is Enlightenment?* September-November 2005, Andrew Cohen remarked to Ken Wilbur: "Interestingly enough, most mortal selves find the notion of living unendingly quite unbearable. Just think about it for a minute. Would Andrew or Ken or anyone else *really* want to live forever as Andrew, Ken, or anyone else? The idea is actually quite terrifying, isn't it?" (pp. 108-09). Connie Barlow agreed. "[I]f someone were to give me the choice to actually download my brain and live forever, or have some sort of nutritional supports so I would live forever, I would absolutely say No. I can't imagine a worse hell" (p. 97).

203 "If our experience of life were to lose its temporality, its unrepeatability, we should soon tire of it, screeching to be relieved of its eternal boredom" (James P. Carse, *The Religious Case Against Belief*, p. 169).

204 *Ibid.*, p. 173.

205 Writing in *The Little Book of Atheist Spirituality,* Andre Comte-Sponville quotes an ancient Greek philosopher's views of mortality: "Epicurus taught us that 'death is nothing.' It is nothing to the living, since as long as they are alive it does not exist; and nothing to the dead, since *they* no longer exist" (p. 7).

206 http://www.allthingsjacq.com/misc_random_quotations.html.

207 Edwin A. Burtt, *Light Love and Life,* pp. 5, 8, 10-11, 105-08. Italics added.

208 *Ibid.*, p. 108.

209 Some Christian theologians have been concerned about the human-like connotations of the word god, and have tried to find terms that are less anthropomorphic. Paul Tillich used phrases such as being-itself, ground of being, and ultimate concern. But these terms lack the emotional punch of that one syllable – *god*. Accord-

ing to Scotty McLennan, Tillich realized that "a neutral, objectifying term like 'It' for God cannot grasp the center of our personality as human beings. Although 'It' might be intellectually correct, the word doesn't include the fullness of faith as a response of one's whole personality: '[I]t cannot overcome our loneliness, anxiety, and despair,' and 'this is the reason that the symbol of the personal God is indispensable for living religion'" (*Jesus Was a Liberal*, p. 59).

210 Daniel C. Dennett, *Breaking the Spell*, p. 272.

211 Christopher Hitchens, *God Is Not Great*, p. 6.

212 Michael Dowd, *Thank God for Evolution,* pp. 30, 120.

213 Anthony Freeman, *God in Us: A Case for Christian Humanism*, p. 2. Another example is the prayer for fair weather: "We humbly beseech thee, that although we for our iniquities have worthily deserved a plague of rain and waters, yet upon our true repentance thou wilt send us such weather, as that we may receive the fruits of the earth in due season . . . ." Freeman translates this prayer in terms of our responsibility for upsetting ecological balance. "We no longer live in a world where natural disasters are understood to be God's punishment for immoral behaviour" (p. 3).

Actually here in America many do still believe that earthquakes and hurricanes are punishments for sin, but people have questioned this idea since ancient times. The Chinese philosopher Lao Tse commented that if lightning expresses the anger of the gods, the gods must be mainly interested in trees!

214 Tom Owen-Towle, *Wrestling With God*, p. 53.

215 Song, "This World is Not My Home," by Albert E. Brumley. Rick Warren comments that "Repeatedly the Bible compares life on earth to temporarily living in a foreign country. This is not your permanent home or final destination" (*The Purpose-Driven Life,* p. 48). This sentiment can affect people's opinions about public policy issues. Geoffrey Fisher, Archbishop of Canterbury, stated that "The hydrogen bomb is not the greatest danger of our time. After all, the most it could do would be to transfer vast numbers of human beings from this world to another and more vital one into which they would

some day go anyway." By this logic it's really no big deal if we all blow ourselves up, obliterating humanity in a thousand Hiroshimas. See http://www.hillmanweb.com/reason/pious_quotes.html.

216 Anthony Freeman, *God in Us: A Case for Christian Humanism*, pp. 52-53, italics deleted.

217 Paul Tillich, *The Courage To Be,* p. 190. Italics are in the original text.

218 Christopher Hitchens, *God Is Not Great*, pp. 151, 153.

219 Teilhard de Chardin, cited by Eric Reitan, *Is God a Delusion?* p. 215.

220 Edwin A. Burtt, *Light Love and Life,* p. 107.

221 Parker Palmer, cited by William R. Murry, *Reason and Reverence*, p. 114. I don't know Palmer's personal beliefs, but Murry, a humanist, endorses Palmer's definition of spirituality.

222 Michael Krasny, *Spiritual Envy,* p. 6.

223 Sam Harris, *Letter to a Christian Nation,* p. 88.

224 Jack Huberman, *The Quotable Atheist*, p. xiv.

225 James Farmalant, *religious humanism*, fall, 2008, p. 73.

226 Jack Huberman, *The Quotable Atheist*, p. 310.

227 Daniel C. Dennett, *Darwin's Dangerous Idea,* p. 520.

228 Sam Harris, *The End of Faith*, p. 41. The Koestler bequest was noted by Jack Huberman, *The Quotable Atheist*, p. 178.

229 Sam Harris, *The End of Faith*, pp. 209, 242.

230 *Ibid.,* p. 234. Italics deleted.

231 Scotty McLennan, *Jesus Was a Liberal*, p. 129.

232 http://www.gallup.com/poll/27682/OneThird-Americans-Beli eve-Bible-Literally-True.aspx.

233 Italics are in the original text. Warren continues, urging his readers to "Resolve that when God says to do something, you will

trust God's Word and do it whether or not it makes sense or you feel like doing it" (Rick Warren, *The Purpose-Driven Life,* p. 187). As you reflect upon the problematic Bible passages we are about to consider, think about whether this is sound advice.

234 Karen Armstrong, *The Case for God*, pp. 326, xv.

235 http://www.infidels.org/library/modern/donald_morgan/inconsi stencies.html.

236 See http://vintage.aomin.org/antitheist_Answers1.html for an argument claiming that this Bible passage has been mistranslated: "The Hebrew term *nacham* is used to express a *range* of meanings, from the idea of 'relenting' or 'repenting' to 'grieving' and 'being sorry.'" See also http://www.songtime.com/bb/bb0106.htm and http://bible.cc/exodus/32-14.htm. However since the story shows Moses trying successfully to make God change his decision, it is not surprising that many translations say God repented.

237 The full text reads, "But if it makes no peace with you, but makes war against you, then you shall besiege it; and when the Lord your God gives it into your hand you shall put all its males to the sword, but the women and the little ones, the cattle, and everything else in the city, all its spoil, you shall take as booty for yourselves; and you shall enjoy the spoil of your enemies, which the Lord your God has given you" (Deuteronomy 20:12-14). Even this sort of forbearance was only extended to faraway cities. In attacking "cities of these peoples that your Lord your God gives you for an inheritance, you shall save alive nothing that breathes . . ." (Deuteronomy 20:16).

238 I once thought Bible passages portraying God as brutal are mostly confined to its first few books. Mark Johnston's *Saving God*, however, makes a more troubling case: "Yahweh's thoroughness in inciting and supporting mass killing is consistent, and extraordinary" (p. 58). The idea that God "is a very dangerous person to mess with . . . is a central theme of the prophetic literature of the Bible. That will be denied, but only by those who have

skipped over, or forgotten, the rather demented reiteration of the theme" (p. 60). Those who play down God's ferocity "underestimate the dramatic character of Yahweh's transformation, his second life as the advocate of justice and compassion" (p. 63).

239 Richard Fuller, cited by Sam Harris, *Letter to a Christian Nation*, p. 17. And Mira Sorvino wonders why it does "not say anywhere in the Bible that slavery is wrong? It only says that you should treat your slaves well. . . . How is it possible that it is not immoral to own another person? Why isn't that one of the Ten Commandments? 'Thou shalt not own another person.' You want to sit here and tell me that fornication is worse than owning someone?" See http://www.celebatheists.com/?title=Mira_Sorvino.

240 For other problematic passages see Leviticus 20:9, Leviticus 21:16-23, Deuteronomy 3:1-6, Deuteronomy 7:2-4, Deuteronomy 22:13-21, Deuteronomy 23:1, Deuteronomy 23:2, Deuteronomy 25:11-12, Joshua 10:40, Judges 11:30-40, Second Kings 2:23-24, Psalms 137:7-9, Proverbs 13:24, Proverbs 22:15, Proverbs 23:13-14, Proverbs 29:15, First Corinthians 11:3-9, and First Timothy 2:11-15. In addition, Ezekiel 18:1-3 and 18:20, Deuteronomy 24:16, and Jeremiah 31:29-30 contradict the inherited-guilt concept of passages such as Deuteronomy 23:2. I am also troubled by Genesis 3:16, Genesis 7:11-24, Genesis 22:1-18, Second Samuel 12:11-18, and Isaiah 13:15, though I know some would defend these passages.

241 Loyal Jones, *The Preacher Joke Book,* p. 72, adapted.

242 Ian S. Markham, *Against Atheism: Why Dawkins, Hitchens, and Harris Are Fundamentally Wrong,* pp. 141-42.

243 Those who favor broad-brush theism include many naturalistic theists, such as those who see God as part of nature but think that science has not yet grasped the essential character of deity.

244 The difference between literal and non-literal theism is a matter of degree. Most literal theists would admit that some god-talk is metaphorical, and most non-literal theists consider some assertions about God to be literally true. For example, one could say that God

is definitely good even if we cannot truly comprehend God's goodness.

245 Since some believers vacillate between relational theism and impartial theism, these two viewpoints may even overlap within the same individual.

246 I placed question-marks in this box and the next one because I am not sure how often relational theism overlaps with theistic physicalism or atheistic physicalism. I call people relational theists if they treat statements about God's personhood as metaphorical, but think that God does relate to us as individuals, e.g., answering our prayers. The beliefs of those relational theists who *very strongly* emphasize metaphor would sometimes overlap with the beliefs of those physicalists who ascribe personal qualities to the material world (either literally or poetically). But does this sort of common ground exist rarely or frequently? To err on the side of caution I marked these boxes "No?"

247 I marked this box and the next one "Yes" because I think there is frequently a lot of overlap between impartial theism and physicalism. Such overlap is especially common among physicalists and impartial theists who emphasize the radically mysterious character of ultimate reality. Many who attain this "higher ignorance" are kindred spirits, even if they disagree about whether to use God-language.

248 In philosophy and theology, post-modernism is a vague term that includes the work of thinkers such as Jacques Derrida, Michel Foucault, and Jean-François Lyotard. Post-modern philosophy typically affirms "a cluster of three ideas: (1) the affirmation of radical and irreducible pluralism . . . (2) the rejection of an overarching metaphysical, or foundational schema . . . and (3) a suspicion of fixed binary categories that describe rigorously separable regions . . ." (John D. Caputo, in *The Cambridge Companion to Atheism,* ed. Michael Martin, p. 268).

249 *Ibid.*, p. 269. Caputo adds that certain post-modernists harbor "a hope or suspicion that there might be some other [a/theological] possibility . . . some hidden future that is concealed from all of us

today." He considers postmodernism "a sustained attempt to displace a fixed categorical opposition of theism and atheism, to make trouble for both traditional religious faith and modern atheism" (p. 279).

INDEX OF NAMES

INDEX OF TOPICS

Made in the USA
Lexington, KY
22 November 2011